Cambridge English

OFFICIAL

ADVANCED 3

WITHOUT ANSWERS

AUTHENTIC EXAMINATION PAPERS

Cambridge University Press
www.cambridge.org/elt

Cambridge Assessment English
www.cambridgeenglish.org

Information on this title: www.cambridge.org/9781108431200

© Cambridge University Press and UCLES 2018

It is normally necessary for written permission for copying to be obtained
in advance from a publisher. The sample answer sheets at the back of this
book are designed to be copied and distributed in class.
The normal requirements are waived here and it is not necessary to write to
Cambridge University Press for permission for an individual teacher to make copies
for use within his or her own classroom. Only those pages that carry the wording
'© UCLES 2018 Photocopiable ' may be copied.

First published 2018

20 19 18 17 16 15 14 13 12 11 10 9 8 7 6 5 4 3 2 1

Printed in Malaysia by Vivar Printing

A catalogue record for this publication is available from the British Library

ISBN 978-1-108-43121-7 Student's Book with answers
ISBN 978-1-108-43122-4 Student's Book with answers with Audio
ISBN 978-1-108-43120-0 Student's Book without answers
ISBN 978-1-108-43123-1 Audio CDs (2)

The publishers have no responsibility for the persistence or accuracy of URLs
for external or third-party internet websites referred to in this publication, and
do not guarantee that any content on such websites is, or will remain, accurate
or appropriate. Information regarding prices, travel timetables, and other factual
information given in this work is correct at the time of first printing but the
publishers do not guarantee the accuracy of such information thereafter.

Contents

Introduction

This collection of four complete practice tests comprises papers from the *Cambridge English: Advanced (CAE)* examination; students can practise these tests on their own or with the help of a teacher.

The *Cambridge English: Advanced* examination is part of a suite of general English examinations produced by Cambridge English Language Assessment. This suite consists of five examinations that have similar characteristics but are designed for different levels of English language ability. Within the five levels, *Cambridge English: Advanced* is at Level C1 in the Council of Europe's *Common European Framework of Reference for Languages: Learning, teaching, assessment.*

It has been accredited by Ofqual, the statutory regulatory authority in England, at Level 2 in the National Qualifications Framework. The *Cambridge English: Advanced* examination is recognised by educational institutions, governmental departments and employers around the world as proof of the ability to follow an academic course of study in English at university level and communicate effectively at a managerial and professional level.

Examination	Council of Europe Framework Level	UK National Qualifications Framework Level
Cambridge English: Proficiency Certificate of Proficiency in English (CPE)	C2	3
Cambridge English: Advanced Certificate in Advanced English (CAE)	C1	2
Cambridge English: First First Certificate in English (FCE)	B2	1
Cambridge English: Preliminary Preliminary English Test (PET)	B1	Entry 3
Cambridge English: Key Key English Test (KET)	A2	Entry 2

The structure of *Cambridge English: Advanced* – an overview

The *Cambridge English: Advanced* examination consists of four papers.

Reading and Use of English   1 hour 30 minutes
This paper consists of **eight** parts, with 56 questions. For Parts 1 to 4, the test contains texts with accompanying grammar and vocabulary tasks, and separate items with a grammar and vocabulary focus. For Parts 5 to 8, the test contains a range of texts and accompanying reading comprehension tasks.

Writing   1 hour 30 minutes
This paper consists of **two** parts which carry equal marks. In Part 1, which is **compulsory**, candidates must write an essay with a discursive focus of between 220 and 260 words. The task requires candidates to write an essay based on two points given in the input text. They need to explain which of the two points is more important and give reasons for their choice.

In Part 2, there are **three** tasks from which candidates **choose one** to write about. The tasks include a letter/email, a proposal, a report and a review. Candidates write between 220 and 260 words in this part.

Listening   40 minutes (approximately)
This paper consists of **four** parts with 30 questions. Each part contains a recorded text or texts and corresponding comprehension tasks. Each part is heard twice.

Speaking   15 minutes
The Speaking test consists of **four** parts. The standard test format is two candidates and two examiners. One examiner acts as both interlocutor and assessor and manages the interaction either by asking questions or providing cues for the candidates. The other acts as assessor and does not join in the conversation. The test consists of short exchanges with the interlocutor and with the other candidate, an individual long turn, a collaborative task involving both candidates, and a discussion.

Grading

Candidates will receive a score on the Cambridge English Scale for each of the four skills and Use of English. The average of these five scores gives the candidate's overall Cambridge English Scale score for the exam. This determines what grade and CEFR level they achieve. All candidates receive a Statement of Results and candidates who pass the examination with Grade A, B or C also receive the *Certificate in Advanced English*. Candidates who achieve Grade A receive the *Certificate in Advanced English* stating that they demonstrated ability at Level C2. Candidates who achieve Grade B or C receive the *Certificate in Advanced English* stating that they demonstrated ability at Level C1. Candidates whose performance is below C1 level, but falls within Level B2, receive a *Cambridge English* certificate stating that they have demonstrated ability at Level B2. Candidates whose performance falls below Level B2 do not receive a certificate.

For further information on grading and results, go to the website (see page 7).

Further information

The information contained in this practice book is designed to be an overview of the exam. For a full description of all of the above exams, including information about task types, testing focus and preparation, please see the relevant handbooks which can be obtained from Cambridge English Language Assessment at the address below or from the website at: www.cambridgeenglish.org

Cambridge English Language Assessment
1 Hills Road
Cambridge CB1 2EU
United Kingdom

Telephone: +44 1223 553997
email: helpdesk@cambridgeenglish.org

Test 1

READING AND USE OF ENGLISH (1 hour 30 minutes)

Part 1

For questions **1–8**, read the text below and decide which answer (**A**, **B**, **C** or **D**) best fits each gap. There is an example at the beginning (**0**).
Mark your answers **on the separate answer sheet**.

Example:

0 A earns   **B** gains   **C** wins   **D** obtained

0	A	B	C	D
	▭	▬	▭	▭

Time and the rotation of the Earth

As all school children know, there are 60 seconds in a minute. But every so often, our planet **(0)** …….. a second. The addition of what's called a 'leap second' is **(1)** …….. to allow the Earth's rotation, which is gradually **(2)** …….. to catch up with atomic clocks – the world's most accurate time-keepers. This sounds simple, but according to scientists, because they only get six months' **(3)** …….. of the need to add a leap second, it's difficult to insert it into computers without mistakes being made, **(4)** …….. systems to fail temporarily. In 2012, a leap second was added on a weekend but it resulted in over 400 flights in one country being grounded as the check-in system **(5)** …….. down.

Some countries are in favour of abolishing leap seconds while others **(6)** …….. that the technical challenges are **(7)** …….. if everyone adds the second in the same way and at the same time. They say that we have always taken the Earth's rotation as the ultimate reference for timekeeping and we shouldn't break this **(8)** …….. without considering the consequences.

1	**A** designed	**B** targeted	**C** framed	**D** drafted
2	**A** delaying	**B** lessening	**C** slowing	**D** declining
3	**A** advice	**B** notice	**C** information	**D** instruction
4	**A** compelling	**B** making	**C** causing	**D** influencing
5	**A** came	**B** fell	**C** ran	**D** went
6	**A** argue	**B** disagree	**C** dispute	**D** question
7	**A** governable	**B** controllable	**C** manageable	**D** adaptable
8	**A** join	**B** link	**C** chain	**D** union

Part 2

For questions **9–16**, read the text below and think of the word which best fits each gap. Use only **one** word in each gap. There is an example at the beginning (**0**).
Write your answers **IN CAPITAL LETTERS on the separate answer sheet.**

Example: | 0 | O | U | T | | | | | | | | | | | | | |

Solving problems while you sleep

How often do we struggle to figure **(0)** .... a problem and then, after a night's sleep, we wake up knowing exactly what to do? We tend to view sleep simply **(9)** .... a period of recuperation, but it actually has profound implications for a lot of human tasks, including a positive effect on problem-solving. Research now suggests that **(10)** .... only are we able to come up with answers to life issues while asleep, but these answers are often better than the ones we might think of once the routines of our daily lives take **(11)** .... Sleep aids memory too, and it's believed that new information isn't processed and absorbed fully until we've had a good night's sleep.

So, if you're faced **(12)** .... a difficult problem, set it aside, sleep **(13)** .... it and return to it the next day. But **(14)** .... made a complex decision, you **(15)** .... like to revisit it after a second night's rest on the off-chance that **(16)** .... could be a better solution waiting to be considered.

Part 3

For questions **17–24**, read the text below. Use the word given in capitals at the end of some of the lines to form a word that fits in the gap **in the same line**. There is an example at the beginning (**0**). Write your answers **IN CAPITAL LETTERS on the separate answer sheet**.

Example:

| 0 | S | I | G | N | I | F | I | C | A | N | C | E | | | | | |

A wise old owl

Many birds have special **(0)** …….. for humans but none is perhaps more respected than the owl. Owls, often seen as symbols of **(17)** …….. , have a powerful hold on human imagination.

SIGNIFY

WISE

There are many species of owl and most of them are solitary, nocturnal birds of prey that are **(18)** …….. by their upright stance. They tend to blend in with the colorations and even the texture patterns of their **(19)** …….. , which makes them hard to spot. They have a keen sense of **(20)** …….. and have special ears that can pick up sounds that are **(21)** …….. by the less sensitive human ear, such as tiny **(22)** …….. from small animals on the ground.

CHARACTER

SURROUND

SEE

DETECT

VIBRATE

Many owls have special feathers on their wings which allow them to fly silently. They are commonly believed to be able to turn their heads a full 360 degrees; in fact, although they have fourteen neck vertebrae in **(23)** …….. with seven in humans, they're only able to rotate 270 degrees.

COMPARE

All these features add to our view of the owl as being **(24)** …….. .

MYSTERY

Part 4

For questions **25–30**, complete the second sentence so that it has a similar meaning to the first sentence, using the word given. **Do not change the word given.** You must use between **three** and **six** words, including the word given. Here is an example (**0**).

Example:

0 James would only speak to the head of department alone.

ON

James ………………………………… to the head of department alone.

The gap can be filled with the words 'insisted on speaking', so you write:

Example:	0	INSISTED ON SPEAKING

Write **only** the missing words **IN CAPITAL LETTERS on the separate answer sheet.**

---

25 If there are fewer doctors on duty, patients may have to wait longer than usual.

DEPENDING

Patients may have to wait longer than usual, …………………………………….... of doctors on duty.

26 There's a danger those mountaineers won't be able to make it back to the hut before it gets dark.

RISK

Those mountaineers run ……………………………….... able to make it back to the hut before it gets dark.

27 Whatever time he leaves home, John always seems to get to work late.

MATTER

No ……………………………….... off from home, John always seems to get to work late.

28 It is Sam's responsibility to ensure everyone has left the museum before closing time.

CHARGE

Sam ………………………….…... sure everyone has left the museum before closing time.

29 Martin was going to host an event for the new students, but it appears he has decided against it.

MIND

Martin appears ………………………….…... hosting an event for the new students.

30 Up to now, I've never thought of working in any field other than finance.

OCCURRED

The thought of not working in the field of finance ………………………….…... now.

Part 5

You are going to read an article in which a young journalist talks about using social media to find a job. For questions **31–36**, choose the answer (**A**, **B**, **C** or **D**) which you think fits best according to the text.

Mark your answers **on the separate answer sheet**.

Keeping pace with scientific publishing

Science correspondent Joe Cushing considers old and new ways of publishing scientific research

Journal-based peer review – the process of subjecting a scientific research paper to the scrutiny of others who are experts in the same field – is generally held up as the quality assurance mechanism for research. It professes to be an essential filter which prevents publishing flawed or nonsensical papers, and indeed is often touted as such in reassuring tones when scientists talk to the media or the general public. Reviewing a paper can delay its publication by up to a year; is that a price worth paying to ensure the trustworthiness of the published literature? Well, yes and no. And picking apart such issues reveals a great deal about the state of scientific publishing, which is very much in flux.

I'm not yet ready to abandon journal-based peer review. I'd still like to see all papers pass some sort of checking stage before formal publication, but I feel the ground moving. The growing use of preprints (drafts of papers which are posted online without having been peer reviewed, found in digital archives) is a crucial part of that shift because they bring academics back to what research publication is all about: the rapid dissemination of new results so they can be read, critiqued and built upon. Publication in journals has become more about renown and career advancement, and this has perverted both the motivations of authors and the job of reviewers.

Competition for prized spots in highly-regarded journals drives scientists to do some of their best work and the best journals certainly publish plenty of outstanding research. But the excessive rewards for publishing in top journals are incentives to corner-cutting, as stories streamlined by the omission of inconvenient data are more likely to be taken up. And the job of the reviewer also becomes distorted: it is more often now to decide, not whether a manuscript is any good, but whether it is good enough for the journal considering publication. For top journals that can depend as much on topicality or newsworthiness as scientific quality.

These problems are well known, but the tragedy for science is that too few people are willing to break away from the present system. However, as the eminent biologist Ron Vale argued recently – fittingly, in a preprint – preprints may be a way out of the impasse because they don't entail a major shift away from the norm. That may seem an odd claim in view of the *line* fact that preprint archives have been in existence for twenty years, yet preprints have not been adopted universally. This slow uptake is not only a reflection of the inherent conservatism of scientists, but also a result of the widespread misconception that journals won't accept manuscripts which have been posted online as preprints. There is also a fear that publication of papers without peer review risks opening the floodgates to 'junk science' – something which, so far at least, has yet to occur. Preprints may not be peer reviewed, but authors know full well that preprints are immediately opened up for critique and discussion by a worldwide community of reviewers.

Tanya Elks, a psychology professor, recalls: 'My paper was a critique of a published paper – a scenario which isn't well handled by the conventional journals. Under their system of anonymous peer reviewing, either the authors of the original paper are chosen as reviewers and there is a risk that the unscrupulous ones might block a critical paper; or they're not chosen and may justifiably complain about misrepresentation. As we posted a preprint, the original authors had their say and we could take their points on board. All the commentary is out in the open so readers can evaluate the quality of the arguments. The possibility of rejection by journals is less of an issue too, given that we'll still have the preprint and comments out in the public domain, so our work won't be wasted.'

Preprint archives enable, on a global scale, the informal *line* scientific discussions once confined to correspondence *line* between individuals. They could also become an *line* effective outlet for negative results – a vital aspect of *line* the scientific process often overlooked by the journals' excessive preoccupation with new discoveries. *line* Furthermore, presence on preprint archives significantly increases the number of times papers are read and cited by others; a potent demonstration of the efficacy *line* of dissemination through preprint. By harnessing *line* the web's culture of openness and accessibility and recalling the collaborative, amateur ethos still at large within the scientific community, preprints should help to refocus attention where it matters – on the work itself, not where it is published.

31 In the first paragraph, the writer expresses doubt regarding the part that peer review plays in

    A provoking changes in the process of scientific publishing.
    B affecting deadlines for publishing scientific papers.
    C ensuring the quality of scientific research.
    D reassuring the public about new research.

32 What does the writer feel that many scientists need to be reminded of?

    A the absence of peer reviewing with preprints
    B the original aim of publishing scientific findings
    C the ulterior motives which lie behind reviewers' comments
    D the prestige which can be gained by being published in a journal

33 What does the writer accuse scientific journals of doing?

    A encouraging scientists to compete against each other
    B trying to reduce costs in order to maintain their position in the market
    C relying too heavily on reviewers to decide whether to publish an article
    D choosing articles for their appeal rather than their scientific value

34 What does the writer admit may be an 'odd claim' in line 45?

    A the idea that it was fitting for biologist Ron Vale to argue his case in a preprint
    B the assertion that adopting preprints does not require a radical change of behaviour
    C the notion that too few scientists are pushing for a rethink of the peer review
    D the suggestion that preprints will be readily accepted by the scientific community

35 What point does Tanya Elks make about her experience of posting a preprint?

    A Her work is less likely to be rejected now since others have made positive comments about it in public.
    B She appreciated the fact that she could see what fellow scientists thought of her paper.
    C It was unfair to use the authors of the research she was evaluating to review her paper.
    D She chose a preprint because she feared her paper would not otherwise be published.

36 The phrase 'collaborative, amateur ethos' in the final paragraph refers back to the earlier phrase

    A 'correspondence between individuals' (lines 75–76).
    B 'effective outlet for negative results' (line 77).
    C 'preoccupation with new discoveries' (line 79).
    D 'efficacy of dissemination' (lines 82–83).

Part 6

You are going to read four commentaries on the subject of living in London. For questions **37–40**, choose from the commentaries **A–D**. The commentaries may be chosen more than once. Mark your answers **on the separate answer sheet**.

London

A Bridget Atkins

London is a cruel city. A quick walk from the steel and glass money temples of the financial district to one of the rundown estates fifteen minutes away shows you most of what you need to know about its harshness and problems. Depressing as that walk may be, I'd still recommend it more than struggling through the public transport network. It isn't just that the trains are overcrowded, overheated and unreliable – it's that you have to pay such an insulting amount for the privilege of travelling in such misery. Talking of contempt, I haven't even got on to landlords, rent, and the fact that a shoebox in London will cost you more than a palace outside London. That's not to say it's all bad though. I do rejoice in the internationalism of my city, the way I learn so much about different cultures and cuisines just by attending a local street party.

B Tim Christie

London is an endlessly inventive city. We've happily embraced using both the London Underground and Overground, cycling and walking, finding one-bed flats further away from the centre. Until now the trend has been to move further out to find a place to live, but it doesn't need to be like that. Some of the most interesting work going on in London now is around the politics of scarcity. We need to release spare space, as well as investigate new models for flexible living and co-housing. People talk about disparities between the haves and the have-nots, but I'd say there's no other place in the world where it's better to be an entrepreneur. You don't have to be born with a silver spoon in your mouth to make it here, and that's what I see – people who are in the process of making it or who already have – just in different places on a kaleidoscopic spectrum.

C Anna Fry

Aside from the fact that most people can no longer afford to live here, there also seems to be a sad conformity among those that do. The big beard, tight-trousered, hipster phenomenon, for instance, is essentially tribal and conservative. I do love the eclectic transport system though. You can make your way across the city by a multitude of transport modes; the whole city is pretty much anti car. Even if you're happy paying the congestion charge, you've still got to drive around in circles looking for a place to park. Get it wrong and there'll be one of London's finest parking attendants there to remind you with the much despised penalty charge notice. But I'm all in favour of that. We all have to breathe the air no matter if we're rich or poor, and that's what I love about the whole system. It's a great equaliser. Take it or leave it.

D Jon Bennett

I don't get the fascination with London's decrepit housing stock. It's overpriced and falling to pieces. All this talk of old-world charm, character and conservation areas, for what is essentially a totally dysfunctional stock of properties not fit for modern-day living. Unless you're a multi-millionaire that is, with money to burn on heating, only for it to go straight out the hundred-year-old windows. Because that's who's drawn here, unless we're talking about the run-down, gritty areas that attract outsiders from all walks of life. If it weren't for them, this would be a dull place to live. I love the way they colonise an area with pop-ups, cafés and art spaces, until they're priced out. The system seems to favour those living off their inheritance. Why else would you need to pay such a ridiculous sum just to get from A to B on a late-running, museum-piece transport system?

Which commentator

expresses a different view from the other three commentators regarding the housing situation in London?

| 37 | |

shares C's opinion on London's public transport system?

| 38 | |

has a different view from A on the multi-cultural nature of London's population?

| 39 | |

shares A's opinion on the inequality of wealth prevalent in London?

| 40 | |

Part 7

You are going to read a magazine article about the ecological importance of the semi-aquatic animal, the beaver. Six paragraphs have been removed from the article. Choose from the paragraphs **A–G** the one which fits each gap (**41–46**). There is one extra paragraph which you do not need to use.

Mark your answers **on the separate answer sheet**.

Beavers

Beavers play an important role in keeping Rhode Island's waters clean

There are an estimated 30 million beavers across North America. As a keystone species, beavers enrich ecosystems around them. By building dams, they control water moving through their habitat, retaining the flow during times of drought and slowing it down during heavy rain and floods. This also creates beaver ponds – areas several meters deep they use for sleeping and eating. However, a study by the American Society of Agronomy says beavers are doing something more: they are now helping to remove nitrogen that has moved its way through soil into ground water and lakes and streams.

41

In time these plants die and decompose, consuming the oxygen from the waters, creating low oxygen levels that kill fish. While these dead zones are common in the Gulf of Mexico, they are also becoming a problem along northeastern U.S. coastlines. However, according to the study findings of Professor Arthur Gold and colleagues of the University of Rhode Island, this problem is less common where there are beavers.

42

Thanks to a naturally occurring bacterium present in the soil of beaver ponds, 5% to 45% of nitrogen in the water can be removed, depending on the pond and the amount of nitrogen present, the study found. This bacterium is able to transform nitrogen in the water into nitrogen gas.

43

This transformative power was tested by taking samples from the beds of beaver ponds, and adding nitrogen to them. These samples were large enough to incorporate the factors that generate the chemical and biological processes that take place in the pond.

44

The experiments also found that 12% of the nitrogen gases created in the samples were nitrous oxide, a very potent greenhouse gas and air pollutant. To put this into perspective, considered over a 100-year period, nitrous oxide is calculated to have between 265 and 310 times more impact than carbon dioxide does. However, the scientists pointed out that the high amount was likely to be a result of some unique laboratory conditions and that it is unlikely these ponds would release that much of the gas in nature.

45

Most of these semi-aquatic animals are in areas with small streams, rather than big rivers, and the beaver dams in these smaller streams are usually the first to be removed. They are considered a nuisance because they block the waterways. This causes a decrease in beaver populations. It is therefore important that these areas remain untouched so they can positively affect nitrogen levels downstream. Professor Gold now hopes to study the ponds over a longer period and to investigate abandoned ponds to see if the nitrogen-retaining qualities remain after the beavers have gone.

46

In addition, these areas of water also attract other wildlife such as insects and birds which are vital to the ecosystem. Studies like the one carried out by Professor Gold may well give people a new-found appreciation for the beaver.

A These results have interesting implications. According to Julia Lazar, who was involved in conducting some of the work as part of her doctoral dissertation and is now working as an environmental consultant, it might change our attitude to beavers and their ponds.

B At the same time, the specimens were also sufficiently small to be easily replicated, managed and measured for numerous changes. The scientists then added a special type of nitrogen to the soil that allowed them to tell if the nitrogen levels were altered and how.

C 'Streamside wetlands are one example of such elements,' said Professor Gold, who studies these types of features in his research. But nobody had ever documented the role beaver ponds might play.

D Found in agricultural fertilizers, nitrogen is often introduced to such areas by runoff, eventually travelling to estuaries where rivers meet the sea. Once in the water system, it has been known to cause what is known as eutrophication. This is where a sudden increase in nutrients can cause blooms of algae to grow.

E This process is known as de-nitrification and means the nitrogen is no longer stored within the stream or pond, and thus can no longer degrade water quality further downstream. However, some of the nitrogen is not changed to gas, but instead is stored in organic soils.

F They are a species whose numbers crashed after widespread hunting 150 years ago, but with their return they are helping solve one of the major problems of the 21st century and that should not be underestimated. It is important to remember that those ponds would not be there without the beavers.

G When the team set out to conduct their research, they quickly realized the water retention time and organic matter build-up within beavers' ponds lead to the creation of ideal conditions for eliminating nitrogen. They then wanted to see how effectively this was done.

Part 8

You are going to read an article in which a squash player writes about the fact that his sport is not included in the Olympic Games. For questions **47–56**, choose from the sections (**A–D**). The sections may be chosen more than once.

Mark your answers **on the separate answer sheet**.

In which section does the writer

say that he's finding it difficult not to express his emotions?	47
express ignorance of certain sports?	48
outline the reasons behind particular decisions?	49
express admiration for some of his colleagues?	50
admit that it had seemed unlikely that his sport would be chosen?	51
acknowledge that he may be repeating a familiar argument?	52
show determination not to be put off his sport by the decision about the Olympics?	53
appear to be asking for advice from the reader?	54
express a fear that people are making fun of his sport?	55
suggest that squash players have had enough of trying to persuade the Olympic committee?	56

The Olympic Games and the sport of squash

Squash player Stuart Lee outlines his reaction to the decision not to include squash in the Olympic Games

A How should I and my fellow squash players react as our sport once again fails to earn a place at the next Olympic Games? With the increasing numbers of international competitions and the recent successful integration of women's and men's tours, one might be forgiven for thinking that the sport has arrived. Except, in Olympic terms, it hasn't. In fact, it's all over the place. For the umpteenth time, squash tried to sell itself and lost. We have pleaded for years and hoped to appeal to a very powerful governing committee responsible for the world's greatest sporting event, and were rejected again. Stop me if you've heard all this before, but over the years, we've dared to think (many times) that we were close to securing Olympic inclusion. Following our latest attempt, five sports were recommended as better options for the next Olympic Games.

B It was always going to be touch-and-go, as the host nation this time around has not traditionally been strong on squash. There was little surprise over the inclusion of baseball and softball – they'll fill arenas and put money in the bank. Surfing is also a fair choice: it's a tough sport, enjoyed by millions of people across the world. But then came sport climbing, and skateboarding. Judging by the reactions I've seen and heard, many people were unaware that such things even existed as sports. Climbing, yes, but what's 'sport climbing'? Do these sports have governing bodies and world titles? Are they televised? Are there rules? Do they have infrastructures and do millions of people do them? I'm not trying to be clever, just asking the questions. Any sport that encourages activity and participation is a great thing, I'm not here to denigrate anything that provides this outlet. I don't know enough about them to say what appeal they would give to the Olympics. Clearly more than squash.

C The official line from both the Professional Squash Association and the World Squash Federation has been extremely gracious, as always. Players have been told not to react negatively, criticise those in charge or lambast other sports, but we're struggling to stop ourselves at this stage. There's some feeling now that it's going to be very hard to keep responding peaceably, merely saying 'Oh well, maybe next time'. Everyone who asks us questions about the Olympics asks with disdain why other sports are selected before squash, and it now seems that disdain has turned to amusement. It was bad enough to play second fiddle to golf and rugby sevens, but at least people who asked for our reaction to those decisions understood that they are established and recognised entities. It has been back-breaking work for squash associations to lobby for inclusion year after year. We've produced swanky and expensive promotional videos with money we didn't have and we have enlisted every celebrity we could get our hands on to hold posters up saying things such as: 'Squash for the Olympics – I'm in – are you?'

D Nobody is quite sure why the sport has suffered these repeated failures. The Olympics is the biggest sporting event in the world. Of course we want to be there, we dearly want to be there but, with respect, all we ever do is try to justify ourselves. Our top players, who are by anyone's standards some of the greatest athletes alive, shouldn't need to do this. This is our sport, it is what it is, and it's getting better all the time. Take it or leave it. We want the Olympics and we hope the Olympics want us. When I heard the news of this latest rejection, I was in the US, playing in an international tournament, and all the players were comforted by the fact that the event had the crowds in raptures every night. It's a fine thing to play in front of such warm and enthusiastic people. The spectators may or may not have heard the news that was on all the players' minds, but squash goes on, Olympics or not.

WRITING (1 hour 30 minutes)

Part 1

You **must** answer this question. Write your answer in **220–260** words in an appropriate style **on the separate answer sheet**.

1 Your class has watched a studio discussion on the role of music in society. You have made the notes below:

> **The role of music in society:**
> - enriching people's lives
> - uniting social groups
> - educating young children

Some opinions expressed in the discussion:

"The purpose of music is to bring beauty to our lives."

"Music can help bring different people together."

"Music lessons at school can improve learning in other subjects."

Write an essay for your tutor discussing **two** of the roles of music in society in your notes. You should **explain which role is more significant, giving reasons** to support your opinion.

You may, if you wish, make use of the opinions expressed in the discussion, but you should use your own words as far as possible.

Part 2

Write an answer to **one** of the questions **2–4** in this part. Write your answer in **220–260** words in an appropriate style **on the separate answer sheet**. Put the question number in the box at the top of the page.

---

2   This is part of an email you have received from your friend Anna in New Zealand:

> ...
>
> I'm doing a project about people's reading habits in different countries. Can you tell me about your country? Can you give me some idea about the situation in your country? What changes have there been in what people read and how they read? Is this the same for all age groups?

    Write your **email**.

3   You have just helped organise a day of activities to welcome new students to the international college where you are a student. The principal has asked you for a report. In your report, you should briefly describe the day, comment on how effective the activities were in welcoming the new students and make recommendations for a similar event next year.

    Write your **report**.

4   Your college website welcomes film reviews from students. You decide to write a review of a science fiction film. In your review, you should briefly describe the film, and consider whether other students would enjoy it. You should also explain how it differs from other popular science fiction films.

    Write your **review**.

LISTENING (approximately 40 minutes)

Part 1

You will hear three different extracts. For questions **1–6**, choose the answer (**A**, **B** or **C**) which fits best according to what you hear. There are two questions for each extract.

Extract One

You hear two friends discussing an exhibition they have just visited, featuring a female sculptor called Sue Lin.

1   What does the woman think about the way the exhibition was set out?

   A It enabled people to appreciate how innovative Sue's work was.

   B It reflected Sue's original intentions for her sculptures.

   C It placed too much emphasis on Sue's contemporaries.

2   The man says the decisions made about what to include in the exhibition have

   A helped to increase visitor numbers.

   B diminished his opinion of Sue's sculptures.

   C disappointed admirers of Sue's talent.

Extract Two

You hear part of a discussion between two psychology students on the subject of laughter.

3   What is the man doing?

   A describing different kinds of humour

   B complaining about his tutor's attitude towards his work

   C highlighting how surroundings can influence people

4   What do they both think about research into laughter?

   A It is an effective way to find out about human behaviour.

   B It should focus on the physical processes of the brain.

   C It has become a popular field of study.

Extract Three

You hear two friends discussing their experiences of learning to play the piano.

5 The woman says that since starting to learn the piano, she's felt

   A more confident about facing challenges in general.

   B newly convinced of the value of perseverance.

   C better able to remember factual information.

6 Which research findings into playing an instrument does the man question?

   A that it improves abstract reasoning skills

   B that it fosters creative thinking

   C that it acts to relieve stress

Part 2

You will hear a book illustrator called Colin Rodgers talking about his work to a group of students. For questions **7–14**, complete the sentences with a word or short phrase.

Colin Rodgers – book illustrator

Colin finds that what particularly holds his attention is the **(7)** .... in

book illustrations.

He advises would-be artists to recognise the importance of continual

(8) .... when they are practising drawing an image.

He finds it hard to capture what he refers to as the **(9)** .... of

a story when he's illustrating it.

He says that children can be more **(10)** .... than adults when

looking at images.

He believes drawings of **(11)** .... in illustrations are readily

understood by everyone.

He gives the example of **(12)** .... as creatures that are easily

placed in any of his pictures.

He stresses the necessity of developing what he terms **(13)** .... in

today's world.

He thinks the quality of **(14)** .... is the most important one for illustrators.

Part 3

You will hear an interview in which a deep-sea map-maker called Sally Gordon and a marine biologist called Mark Tomkins are talking about making maps of the ocean floor. For questions **15–20**, choose the answer (**A**, **B**, **C** or **D**) which fits best according to what you hear.

15 How did Sally feel when she had completed her first mapping expedition?
   A anxious about the prospect of spending more time at sea
   B unsure whether she had made a good impression
   C keen to begin making a reputation as a leader
   D excited at the prospect of making further discoveries

16 Mark compares the ocean floor to the planets in order to
   A emphasise how under-explored it is.
   B reassess its geographical features.
   C challenge assumptions about the practical difficulties of researching it.
   D speculate about the extent of the area it covers.

17 How does Sally feel about attitudes towards deep-sea exploration?
   A glad that its importance is recognised
   B frustrated that it's not regarded with more enthusiasm
   C optimistic about the possibility of gaining support for it
   D disappointed by public misunderstanding of it

18 They agree that corporate funding of science projects
   A appeals to an idealistic kind of entrepreneur.
   B is now more popular than sports sponsorship.
   C generates a lot of positive publicity for companies.
   D leads to more accurate results than government funding.

19 When talking about the territorial ambitions of some island nations, Mark reveals his
   A irritation at their lack of scientific know-how.
   B support for their right to claim what's theirs.
   C scepticism about the legality of the process.
   D concern about the potential consequences.

20 Sally and Mark predict that future developments in deep-sea exploration will
   A result in a change in human behaviour.
   B help to raise the profile of marine biology.
   C enable a new form of tourism to come into being.
   D have a bigger impact than those in space exploration.

Part 4

You will hear five short extracts in which people are talking about going to live in another country.

TASK ONE

For questions **21–25**, choose from the list (**A–H**) what each speaker's main reason for moving to the new country.

TASK TWO

For questions **26–30**, choose from the list (**A–H**) what each speaker was surprised each speaker about the place where they are now living.

While you listen, you must complete both tasks.

	TASK ONE		TASK TWO	
A	to satisfy a desire for change		differences in language use	
B	to take the advice of a friend	Speaker 1 21	a seasonal abnormality	Speaker 1 26
C	to have a chance no longer possible at home	Speaker 2 22	the national cuisine	Speaker 2 27
D	to achieve a long-standing ambition	Speaker 3 23	practical difficulties of daily life	Speaker 3 28
E	to accompany someone else	Speaker 4 24	the contrast in working cultures	Speaker 4 29
F	to improve a particular skill	Speaker 5 25	people's sense of humour	Speaker 5 30
G	to be part of an important trend		the attitude of local people	
H	to take advantage of an unexpected opportunity		the authentic reconstructions	

SPEAKING (15 minutes)

There are two examiners. One (the interlocutor) conducts the test, providing you with the necessary materials and explaining what you have to do. The other examiner (the assessor) is introduced to you, but then takes no further part in the interaction.

Part 1 (2 minutes)

The interlocutor first asks you and your partner for some information about yourselves, then widens the scope of the questions by asking about e.g. your leisure activities, studies, travel and daily life. You are expected to respond to the interlocutor's questions and listen to what your partner has to say.

Part 2 (a one-minute 'long turn' for each candidate, plus a 30-second response from the second candidate)

You are each given the opportunity to talk for about a minute, and to comment briefly after your partner has spoken.

The interlocutor gives you a set of three pictures and asks you to talk about two of them for about one minute. It is important to listen carefully to the interlocutor's instructions. The interlocutor then asks your partner a question about your pictures and your partner responds briefly.

You are then given another set of pictures to look at. Your partner talks about these pictures for about one minute. This time the interlocutor asks you a question about your partner's pictures and you respond briefly.

Part 3 (4 minutes)

In this part of the test, you and your partner are asked to talk together. The interlocutor places a question and some text prompts on the table between you. This stimulus provides the basis for a discussion, after which you will need to make a decision on the topic in question. The interlocutor explains what you have to do.

Part 4 (5 minutes)

The interlocutor asks some further questions, which leads to a more general discussion of the topic you have discussed in Part 3. You may comment on your partner's answers if you wish.

Test 2

READING AND USE OF ENGLISH (1 hour 30 minutes)

Part 1

For questions **1–8**, read the text below and decide which answer (**A**, **B**, **C** or **D**) best fits each gap. There is an example at the beginning (**0**).
Mark your answers **on the separate answer sheet**.

Example:

0 A crammed   **B** crushed   **C** massed   **D** piled

0	A	B	C	D
	▬	▭	▭	▭

Reading the slow way

It's 7 pm and I'm sitting in a café I've never been in before. It's **(0)** .... with people, but nobody's talking. Nothing **(1)** .... about this in a big city, but we're not just sitting there ignoring each other. **(2)** .... the opposite; we're all reading together, silently, in a 'Slow Reading Club', an idea from New Zealand. **(3)** .... our lives, clearing some mental **(4)** .... where our attention is not constantly divided between ten different things is the trend of the moment, but it's not easy to **(5)** ....

The Slow Reading Club aims to meet that challenge by encouraging people to apply the same discipline to reading as to going to the gym or completing a task at work. The rules are **(6)** .... straightforward: bring a book and **(7)** .... yourself in it the way you did as a child. I've brought a thriller which has lain **(8)** .... on my bookshelves for years. At the end of our hour, we're told it's time to stop reading and it feels like emerging from a deep sleep. I'm off home to carry on reading.

1   **A** contrary   **B** abnormal   **C** variable   **D** disparate

2   **A** Fully   **B** Thoroughly   **C** Wholly   **D** Quite

3   **A** Simplifying   **B** Relieving   **C** Moderating   **D** Relaxing

4   **A** place   **B** span   **C** space   **D** area

5   **A** deliver   **B** attain   **C** perform   **D** acquire

6   **A** exactly   **B** rather   **C** thereby   **D** somewhat

7   **A** lose   **B** place   **C** concentrate   **D** free

8   **A** negated   **B** deserted   **C** declined   **D** neglected

Part 2

For questions **9–16**, read the text below and think of the word which best fits each gap. Use only **one** word in each gap. There is an example at the beginning (**0**).
Write your answers **IN CAPITAL LETTERS on the separate answer sheet**.

Example:

0		T	O																

Discovering new material

Vulcanised rubber, celluloid and plastic – these materials were, **(0)** .... a certain degree, invented by accident. In fact, the history of materials can be described **(9)** .... a history of accidents, but this is not as catastrophic as it sounds. **(10)** .... the beginning of scientific investigation, scientists have stumbled across new and wonderful materials in **(11)** .... course of exploring something completely different. But this chance discovery of useful materials **(12)** .... undergoing a change.

Scientists sitting at their desks, now turn to computers to design materials and to work out their properties long **(13)** .... they need to go anywhere near a laboratory. But the element of chance is still present as the ultimate application of these new materials remains tentative. **(14)** .... scientists are confident about is that each has the potential to be revolutionary. The race is now on to make these materials reality. **(15)** .... the history of materials is any guide, how we eventually use them will, **(16)** .... part, be discovered accidentally.

Part 3

For questions **17–24**, read the text below. Use the word given in capitals at the end of some of the lines to form a word that fits in the gap **in the same line**. There is an example at the beginning (**0**). Write your answers **IN CAPITAL LETTERS on the separate answer sheet**.

Example:

| 0 | A | P | P | R | E | N | T | I | C | E | S | H | I | P | | | | |

"Mouseman"

The furniture maker, Robert Thompson, was born in 1876. As a young
man he started an engineering **(0)** .... He described this time   **APPRENTICE**
as like a prison sentence with harsh, **(17)** .... conditions. This   **TOLERATE**
experience resulted in him taking the decision to work **(18)** .... his   **ALONG**
father, who was making handcrafted oak furniture following traditional
methods. Following his father's death in 1895, Robert was left with full
(19) .... for the family business.   **RESPONSE**

The company decided to include a **(20)** .... of a mouse on all   **CARVE**
its items of furniture as a sort of logo. This gave Thompson the
nickname, "Mouseman", which remains the **(21)** .... trademark of his   **DISTINCT**
company's furniture.

Time-honoured methods are still used for the **(22)** .... of the furniture   **ASSEMBLE**
and any upholstery is always made of the highest quality leather,
(23) .... to water and other stains. The company is still run by the   **RESIST**
Mouseman's **(24)** .... , and now enjoys worldwide distribution of   **DESCEND**
its products.

Part 5

You are going to read a newspaper article about food. For questions **31–36**, choose the answer (**A**, **B**, **C** or **D**) which you think fits best according to the text.
Mark your answers **on the separate answer sheet**.

The food scientist
Alice Baines meets the influential food scientist Charles Spence

Charles Spence will eat just about anything. 'We've got ice cream made from bee larvae at home,' says the Professor of Experimental Psychology in his office at Oxford
line 4   University in the UK. They may be maggoty in appearance, but they apparently have a 'slightly nutty, floral' flavour. How to make bug-eating acceptable is just one of the
line 7   many gustatory challenges that Spence and his team are tackling. Through his studies into how the senses interact to form our perception of flavour, Spence is influencing,
line 10   in a stealthy but not inconsiderable manner, what we eat
line 11   and drink, from the hefty output of food-industry giants (he sits on the scientific advisory board of one well-known multinational conglomerate, and receives funding from another), to the menus of leading restaurants.

Spence and his peers have, through a line of scientific inquiry that is informally referred to as gastro physics, studied in minute detail how we experience food and drink. Who we eat with; how food is arranged and described; the colour, texture and weight of plates and cutlery; background noise – all these things affect taste. Spence's book, *The Perfect Meal*, written with Betina Piqueras-Fiszman, is packed with insights that are fascinating to anyone in possession of an appetite.

Were you aware that the person in a group who orders first in a restaurant enjoys their food most? And did you realise that we consume about 35% more food when eating with one other person, rising to 75% more when dining with three others?

Spence's lab in Oxford is noticeably un-space-age. 'Low-tech, paper and drawing pin stuff,' he readily admits. There are soundproof booths that resemble human-sized safes ('most of my PhD was done in one of those,' he says fondly), along with stacks of ancient-looking audio-visual equipment. By keeping overheads low, he can afford to work more creatively with cooks who can't fund academic research themselves. Much of his work is funded by a major food multinational. Historically, he says, undertaking research which attracts industry funding has been seen in university circles as 'what you do if you can't do proper science'. But since the government insisted that universities demonstrate their work has an impact and that people are interested in it, this type of research has become a strategically good thing to do.

Spence is currently helping famous brands through (often government-imposed) reductions in salt and sugar. It is in their interests, he points out, to help loyal customers stay alive for longer. Perhaps surprisingly, many have been making these reductions furtively, behind closed doors. They do it gradually, so regular consumers don't notice the difference from one pack to the next. 'The research shows that when you tell people what you're doing, it makes them focus on the taste and for whatever reason they don't like it as much,' he says.

It was while working on a project for a major food producer that Spence was first introduced to Heston Blumenthal, the renowned experimental chef. 'At the time, people thought: "Science and food – that's horrible," although most food is scientific, in fact. Who better to change the mindset than Heston?' It was through Blumenthal's collaborations with Spence, who had been studying the effects of sound on flavour, that the 'Sound of the Sea' dish came about in Blumenthal's five-star restaurant. Interestingly, Spence says that members of the early-twentieth-century art movement, the Italian futurists, were 'doing sounds of croaking frogs with frogs' legs a century ago', but that it didn't catch on.

Now the food industry is applying Spence's sensory science to products left, right and centre. This includes his recent findings that higher-pitched music enhances sweetness, and lower-pitched and brassy sounds make food taste bitter. 'It's always surprising when shapes affect taste, or when a tune can impact on how you perceive a flavour,' he says. An airline will soon be matching music with food served to passengers. And last year, a well-known brand released a smartphone app that plays a concerto while your ice cream softens; they omitted to match the music to the taste, though, which is all too frequently the case according to Spence.

What, one wonders, are dinner parties like in the Spence household? There was the time they ate rabbit, with the fur wrapped around the cutlery. And the one at which they played with remote-controlled, multi-coloured light bulbs. 'We've had dinner parties with a tone generator, headphones and ten different drinks lined up to see whether they have different pitches.' Home, sweet shops, food conventions, international gastronomy conferences: they're all extensions of the lab to Spence.

31 Which word in the first paragraph is used to indicate distaste?

    A maggoty (line 4)
    B gustatory (line 7)
    C stealthy (line 10)
    D hefty (line 11)

32 What does the writer suggest about Spence's work in the fourth paragraph?

    A Small-scale projects have brought it most success.
    B It is less forward-looking than might be expected.
    C Perceptions of its value have changed.
    D It suffers from inadequate resources.

33 What point does Spence make about major food companies in the fifth paragraph?

    A They should pay less attention to public opinion.
    B They will benefit in the long term from selling healthier goods.
    C They are reluctant to invest in developing new products.
    D They have been too secretive about the way they work.

34 Spence's view of Heston Blumenthal is one of

    A enthusiasm for his links with innovators from the past.
    B admiration for his influence on ways of thinking about food.
    C fascination for his involvement with large food manufacturers.
    D respect for his thorough knowledge of science.

35 Spence is concerned that his ideas

    A are being developed in unexpected ways.
    B seem too challenging to be widely accepted.
    C appear to attract the wrong sort of organisations.
    D are often applied in a way that neglects some details.

36 What does the final paragraph highlight about Spence?

    A the commitment he shows to his research
    B the unpredictable nature of his character
    C the talent he has for entertaining people
    D the busy daily schedule he follows

Part 7

You are going to read a newspaper article about a holiday in Costa Rica. Six paragraphs have been removed from the article. Choose from the paragraphs **A–G** the one which fits each gap (**41–46**). There is one extra paragraph which you do not need to use.
Mark your answers **on the separate answer sheet**.

Costa Rican holiday

Not again. It's the third morning in succession we've been woken by howler monkeys. The noise invades your consciousness like some distant wind and builds into a sustained roar until you fling off the sheets and sit up, cursing. Awake, you can hear the throaty rasp. The volume is astonishing: this is reputedly the loudest voice on the planet yet it comes from an animal no larger than a cat.

41

Later on that morning, strapped into harness and helmet and slightly regretting my immense breakfast, I find myself standing on a narrow platform overlooking the forested gorge. A steel cable arcs down through the trees to some invisible point on the other side. This seems the last chance to voice my fears, were it not for the fact that my nine-year-old daughter is already clipped on ahead of me. The last thing I see as she launches into the void is her grin.

42

As I zigzag down from platform to platform I can relax enough to appreciate the gurgle of the river and the chorus of birdsong. There is even time to spot a troop of howler monkeys in the crown of a fig tree. By the time we swing off the final platform, fun has definitely conquered fear.

43

'They control our climate,' our guide Daniel Monge had told us on day one. He had showed us on our map how Costa Rica's peaks line up to form a barrier down the spine of the country. The eastern slopes, which fall away to the Caribbean,

get most of the rainfall and are carpeted in lush tropical rainforest. The western Pacific slopes lie in the rain shadow, so their forests are more arid.

44

By afternoon, the skies had cleared, giving us picture-book views of Turrialba, the next volcano on our route. An ominous plume of smoke rose from the summit, and the Lodge, our stop for the night, was directly below. 'Don't worry,' said Daniel, 'it's been doing that for three years.'

45

From that experience to watching how sugar was made seemed a natural leap. We joined a group to watch as the estate's two oxen turned a huge mill wheel that crushed fresh cane to a sticky pulp. The children's eyes widened as the first fresh juice was boiled up into a slow-bubbling gloop of golden molasses, then the raw sugar was spread, chopped and sifted.

46

For our last two days, we descended from Rincón de la Vieja to our hotel in Playa Panama. It turns out to be perfect: the lush grounds, the huge pool, the lavish breakfast and the warm ocean just beyond. How better to wind down before the flight home? There's only one problem, and it comes at 5.03 am on our final morning: a thunderous wake-up call courtesy of the planet's noisiest primates. I pull my pillow over my ears.

A Our next stop was on neither of these, however, but in the misty highlands that divide them. We drove up a hairpin ascent to Costa Rica's highest active volcano. On a good day, you can see both coasts from here. We had no such luck, but the swirling mist allowed glimpses into the flooded crater.

B Still, an early start is no bad thing. So far, we've needed every minute of daylight to get through our breathless itinerary, and our time at this guest house promises to be the most action-packed yet.

C That evening, inspired by what we'd seen, we cooked our own Costa Rican meal. Our hosts provided ingredients and instructions, and then kept a discreet distance as we sliced, mashed, drizzled and seasoned to produce our best shot at a traditional supper.

D But you don't need a guide to find Costa Rica's wildlife. In fact, you don't even need to go looking for it. So exuberant is nature in this part of the world that wild creatures form an unavoidable backdrop to whatever else you might get up to.

E The next morning, with these anxieties having proved unfounded, we wound further down through the coffee plantations in the sunshine to the estate of Tayutic. Here, my daughter helped to sort good macadamia nuts from bad as they rattled down the chute, then attempted to crush dried coffee beans in a stone mill.

F Admittedly, this would feel even more daunting if we hadn't done this already a few days ago, on the slopes of Arenal Volcano. Then, I found it terrifying, hurtling at unnatural speeds high above the canopy. Now I'm a little more confident.

G But before I can glory in my success, we're making our way to a hot springs resort, the penultimate stop on our two-week Costa Rican adventure tour. Like the other volcanoes we've seen in the country, the one near here belches sulphurous smoke.

WRITING (1 hour 30 minutes)

Part 1

You **must** answer this question. Write your answer in **220–260** words in an appropriate style **on the separate answer sheet**.

---

1   Your class has listened to a radio discussion about the benefits of learning languages. You have made the notes below:

Benefits of learning languages:
- understanding other cultures
- increasing job opportunities
- providing intellectual challenge

Some opinions expressed in the discussion:

"When you learn a language you learn a lot more than just words."

"You can apply for great jobs if you speak other languages."

"Learning languages is good for the brain."

Write an essay for your tutor discussing **two** of the benefits of learning languages in your notes. You should **explain which benefit is more important, giving reasons** to support your opinion.

You may, if you wish, make use of the opinions expressed in the discussion, but you should use your own words as far as possible.

Part 2

Write an answer to **one** of the questions **2–4** in this part. Write your answer in **220–260** words in an appropriate style **on the separate answer sheet**. Put the question number in the box at the top of the page.

---

2   A TV company, FileView TV, is planning to produce a series 'The World's Greatest Sports Personalities of All Time'. They would like viewers to send in proposals suggesting someone to feature in the series. Say who you would suggest, describe that person's contribution to their sport, and explain whether or not the person is a good role model for today's young people.

Write your **proposal**.

3   You are a student at an international college. You have decided to write to the college principal to suggest that the college should start a bus service for the college. In your letter, you should describe the problems of travelling to and from college, explain the reasons for your suggestion, and assess the benefits for the college and the local area.

Write your **letter. You do not need to include postal addresses.**

4   You have just completed three months of unpaid work experience in a large company to learn about a career you are interested in. The company director has asked you to write a report. In your report, you should describe the new skills you acquired, comment on how well you were supported by the people you worked with, and evaluate how useful the experience will be for your future career.

Write your **report.**

Part 2

You will hear a sports nutritionist called Emily Anderson talking to a group of students about how she helps young athletes with their diet. For questions **7–14**, complete the sentences with a word or short phrase.

Working as a sports nutritionist

Emily's early passion for **(7)** .... influenced her choice of career.

After completing her education, Emily wanted to find employment in

(8) .... but there was a lack of opportunity.

Emily uses the word **(9)** .... to describe the stage youth

athletics has reached.

Emily often leads **(10)** .... , which she finds very rewarding.

Emily recommends doing a degree module in **(11)** .... to

increase work opportunities.

Emily explains that reading **(12)** .... the best way to keep

up with the latest developments.

Emily points out that what she calls the **(13)** .... can require

considerable investment.

Emily was surprised that one of the advantages of her job is the **(14)** ....

that she can use.

Part 3

You will hear part of an interview with two environmentalists, Carol Jones and James Wilson, who are talking about an approach to conservation called rewilding, and damaged environments. For questions **15–20**, choose the answer (**A**, **B**, **C** or **D**) which fits best according to what you hear.

15 Carol's view of rewilding as a form of conservation is that it
    A   is limited in its scope.
    B   enables native species to thrive.
    C   is often misunderstood by non-scientists.
    D   may be difficult to implement with some species.

16 James supports the presence of alien species because
    A   they have been shown to improve soil quality.
    B   they are part of the evolution of nature.
    C   the problem of removing them is too complex.
    D   most native species are too weak to survive.

17 Carol produced her report on the location of native species in order to
    A   contradict certain widely-held beliefs.
    B   criticise the way people neglect nature.
    C   provide support for her original hypothesis.
    D   enable research to be done into unusual habitats.

18 With conservation work, Carol and James both think that
    A   it's easy to learn from past mistakes made with ecosystems.
    B   most ecosystems today have undergone some improvement.
    C   it's necessary to understand that all ecosystems are dynamic.
    D   most people accept the idea that climate change affects ecosystems.

19 Why does Carol mention wildlife corridors?
    A   to illustrate what ordinary citizens can do
    B   to clarify a scientific term that is often misunderstood
    C   to describe the way animals behave in urban environments
    D   to show why open spaces have disappeared from cities

20 How does James feel about the attitude of some people towards the environment?
    A   worried about the way they ignore the problems
    B   annoyed that they are unwilling to listen to suggestions
    C   frustrated that they continue to plant non-native species
    D   disappointed that they are only concerned with their own interests

Part 4

You will hear five short extracts in which people are talking about leaving their previous jobs to work freelance from home.

TASK ONE

For questions **21–25**, choose from the list (**A–H**) the reason why each speaker decided to work freelance from home.

TASK TWO

For questions **26–30**, choose from the list (**A–H**) the aspect of working freelance from home which each speaker has found challenging.

While you listen, you must complete both tasks.

TASK ONE		TASK TWO	
A to fulfil a greater variety of tasks		A resisting online distractions	
B to feel free of supervision	Speaker 1 [ ] [21]	B having no colleagues to talk to	Speaker 1 [ ] [26]
C to follow the example of a friend	Speaker 2 [ ] [22]	C stopping focussing on work at the end of the day	Speaker 2 [ ] [27]
D to develop their creativity	Speaker 3 [ ] [23]	D feeling responsible for everything	Speaker 3 [ ] [28]
E to gain greater financial rewards	Speaker 4 [ ] [24]	E keeping up with professional developments	Speaker 4 [ ] [29]
F to avoid travel difficulties	Speaker 5 [ ] [25]	F organising the physical workspace	Speaker 5 [ ] [30]
G to be in control of their workload		G receiving no feedback from superiors	
H to have more options for holidays		H preventing interruptions from visitors	

SPEAKING (15 minutes)

There are two examiners. One (the interlocutor) conducts the test, providing you with the necessary materials and explaining what you have to do. The other examiner (the assessor) is introduced to you, but then takes no further part in the interaction.

Part 1 (2 minutes)

The interlocutor first asks you and your partner for some information about yourselves, then widens the scope of the questions by asking about e.g. your leisure activities, studies, travel and daily life. You are expected to respond to the interlocutor's questions and listen to what your partner has to say.

Part 2 (a one-minute 'long turn' for each candidate, plus a 30-second response from the second candidate)

You are each given the opportunity to talk for about a minute, and to comment briefly after your partner has spoken.

The interlocutor gives you a set of three pictures and asks you to talk about two of them for about one minute. It is important to listen carefully to the interlocutor's instructions. The interlocutor then asks your partner a question about your pictures and your partner responds briefly.

You are then given another set of pictures to look at. Your partner talks about these pictures for about one minute. This time the interlocutor asks you a question about your partner's pictures and you respond briefly.

Part 3 (4 minutes)

In this part of the test, you and your partner are asked to talk together. The interlocutor places a question and some text prompts on the table between you. This stimulus provides the basis for a discussion, after which you will need to make a decision on the topic in question. The interlocutor explains what you have to do.

Part 4 (5 minutes)

The interlocutor asks some further questions, which leads to a more general discussion of the topic you have discussed in Part 3. You may comment on your partner's answers if you wish.

Test 3

READING AND USE OF ENGLISH (1 hour 30 minutes)

Part 1

For questions **1–8**, read the text below and decide which answer (**A, B, C** or **D**) best fits each gap. There is an example at the beginning (**0**).
Mark your answers **on the separate answer sheet**.

Example:

0 A regard   **B** notice   **C** recognise   **D** watch

0	A	B	C	D
	▭	▭	▭	▬

Glass

Over 400 years ago, the Italian inventor, Galileo, became the first person in history to use a telescope to **(0)** …….. the night sky and see the solar system in all its **(1)** …….. . This was possible because Europeans were already using glass, for example to make windows and elaborate chandeliers, and were well aware of its **(2)** …….. . So when Galileo decided he wanted a telescope, he had a **(3)** …….. tradition of glassmaking and highly skilled glassmakers who he could **(4)** …….. on to provide him with a lens.

Glass lenses were later **(5)** …….. to many other uses, not least the invention of eye glasses. It's hard to **(6)** …….. the impact of this technology on those who up to that point could only see a blurred world.

Yet for all its considerable importance in human history, glass is now taken for granted. When we go to the top of a skyscraper we **(7)** …….. the quality of the light but rarely the glass itself. Perhaps it's because we look through it, rather than at it, that glass fails to **(8)** …….. to our emotions.

1   **A** marvel   **B** glory   **C** magic   **D** triumph

2   **A** aspects   **B** means   **C** properties   **D** resources

3   **A** fruitful   **B** deep   **C** plentiful   **D** rich

4   **A** catch   **B** hold   **C** call   **D** pick

5   **A** put   **B** taken   **C** set   **D** turned

6   **A** overcome   **B** overstate   **C** overtake   **D** overdo

7   **A** approve   **B** compliment   **C** honour   **D** appreciate

8   **A** demand   **B** appeal   **C** claim   **D** attract

Part 2

For questions **9–16**, read the text below and think of the word which best fits each gap. Use only **one** word in each gap. There is an example at the beginning (**0**).
Write your answers **IN CAPITAL LETTERS on the separate answer sheet**.

Example: | **0** | A | R | O | U | N | D | | | | | | | | | | |

Handwriting is history

Handwriting has been **(0)** .... for about 6,000 years, just a small fraction of the time that humans have been on this earth, but its effects have been enormous. Writing doesn't come naturally to us; **(9)** .... seeing and hearing, it must be taught.

However, **(10)** .... that computers have taken over our world, the need to write anything by hand is becoming redundant. Some educationalists are therefore questioning why schools should teach joined-up writing at **(11)** .... It takes up a lot of teaching time that could otherwise be devoted **(12)** .... keyboard skills. But these experts admit that handwriting **(13)** .... indeed have a presence that is absent in typed prose.

Many of us rebel **(14)** .... the radical idea of abandoning writing by hand because we think that our personal identity shines through in our handwriting. It allows self-expression to grow and is regarded by many **(15)** .... the mark of a civilised society. So, are we really ready to enter a world **(16)** .... the artistic flow of handwritten script might be about to disappear?

Part 3

For questions **17–24**, read the text below. Use the word given in capitals at the end of some of the lines to form a word that fits in the gap **in the same line**. There is an example at the beginning (**0**). Write your answers **IN CAPITAL LETTERS on the separate answer sheet**.

Example:

| **0** | B | E | N | E | F | I | C | I | A | L | | | | | | | |

Singing in a choir is good for you!

According to researchers, not only does singing in a choir make us feel good, it may also be **(0)** .... to our health.   **BENEFIT**

A recent online survey of people who sang in choirs, played team sports or took up dancing all yielded very high levels of **(17)** ....   **PSYCHOLOGY** well-being. However, it was the choristers who stood out as feeling the most **(18)** .... Why is this? Singing in a choir was shown   **LIFT** to be **(19)** .... more effective at improving the mood of its   **SIGNIFY** **(20)** .... because of the synchronised moving and breathing with   **PARTICIPATE** other people. Alternatively, it could simply be the fact that being part of a **(21)** .... group is particularly satisfying. Over the years,   **MEAN** researchers have found that choral singing has a number of health benefits as well, including boosting the immune system and lowering stress levels. One study has even suggested that it can increase life **(22)** ....   **EXPECT**

Although researchers admit that some of their studies are still **(23)** .... , they feel there does seem to be the   **SPECULATE** **(24)** .... that singing in a group is more than just fun.   **IMPLY**

Part 4

For questions **25–30**, complete the second sentence so that it has a similar meaning to the first sentence, using the word given. **Do not change the word given.** You must use between **three** and **six** words, including the word given. Here is an example (**0**).

Example:

0 James would only speak to the head of department alone.

ON

James ………………………………… to the head of department alone.

The gap can be filled with the words 'insisted on speaking', so you write:

Example:	0	INSISTED ON SPEAKING

Write **only** the missing words **IN CAPITAL LETTERS on the separate answer sheet.**

---

25 I'm convinced that David is holding something back about his plans for moving.

   HONEST

   I'm convinced that David is …………………………………….... about his plans for moving.

26 John always trained hard, but he never succeeded in winning a gold medal.

   HOW

   No ……………………………….... trained, he never succeeded in winning a gold medal.

27 The manager assured me that she would order a replacement watch.

   WORD

   The manager …………………………………….... that she would order a replacement watch.

28 There was no money to allow the construction of the road to continue.

LACK

Construction of the road could not …………………………….... money.

29 The manager never doubted that the latest model of the phone would be a great success.

MIND

There was never any …………………………….... that the latest model of the phone would be a great success.

30 Gina found it impressive that her tutor was able to remember all his students' names.

ABILITY

Gina was …………………………….... to remember all his students' names.

Part 5

You are going to read an article about philosophy. For questions **31–36**, choose the answer (**A**, **B**, **C** or **D**) which you think fits best according to the text.
Mark your answers **on the separate answer sheet**.

Philosophy needs to engage more with the world

Philosopher Adrian Small considers the role of philosophers in modern life

'What do you do for a living?' It's classic small talk – we define ourselves by our jobs. And it's a question usually answered in a few words. However, when you're a philosopher, as I am, it's slightly harder to deal with. For one thing, describing yourself as a philosopher sounds rather pretentious. Saying you study or teach the subject is fine, but to say you are a philosopher is, in the eyes of many, to claim access to some mystical truth or enlightenment above one's fellows. This is clearly nonsense; philosophers are no different from – indeed are part of – the masses, but the persistence of the notion makes me hesitate.

So why does this stereotype of a philosopher pervade? One reason is that philosophers have established themselves as people who judge the activities of others and celebrate intellectual life. The Greek philosopher Aristotle (384 – 322 BC) argued that a life lived in contemplation, i.e. a philosophical life, was the most virtuous of all. Few modern philosophers would agree, but there's still a cultural aura around philosophy that associates it, rightly, with the life of the mind. Another Greek philosopher, Socrates, remarked that 'the unexamined life is not worth living', meaning that a life that simply accepted prevailing cultural norms would be deeply unsatisfying. It's partly mankind's innate ability to reflect upon the world that allows us control over our lives, and therefore the ability to make our own decisions.

But the examined life doesn't require the wide reading of the philosophical classics, nor a life dedicated to intellectual reflection. It simply means looking more closely at the everyday experiences that define our lives to ensure they deserve their central role. It doesn't need to be the life of the sage, removed from society in order to evaluate it impartially. In fact, in order for the examined life to serve in guiding the experience of individuals, it's actually a deeply practical enterprise, and one in which knowledge should be shared, as it's an essential element of the good life.

This brings me to a second reason for the misconception about philosophers: in becoming a profession, academic philosophy has grown increasingly removed from lived experiences, especially those of people without formal training in the discipline. This isn't entirely the fault of philosophers: university funding, performance evaluations and esteem are tied to increasingly expensive and inaccessible academic journals. As a result, philosophers have little opportunity to explain their ideas to anyone other than the minute group of experts who populate their particular field of study. For the lay observer, the discipline can often seem far removed from reality.

If the bulk of philosophers once challenged this view of themselves as being remote, many have since ceased. Although the university system initiated the environment of privileged isolation, academics haven't shied away from supporting it. As thinking in some areas has grown increasingly concerned with very specific, technical debates, the process of interpreting them for philosophers working outside the specific subfield can be laborious enough, but trying to do so for the untrained mind becomes almost impossible. Philosophy, in some circles, has withdrawn from society altogether. This trend must be reversed.

I sometimes describe myself as an 'ethicist', because most of my work is in ethics, the field of philosophy concerned with evaluating human activity. More recently, though, I've begun to feel that title insufficient to capture my area of inquiry, because ethics is commonly asserted as being connected to formal codes, values and laws. This represents quite a new and largely unconsidered development in philosophical thinking: the field of ethics has colloquially come to refer to applied ethics – a subfield that explores the justice of particular social practices. The task of the ethicist, in modern thinking, is to determine whether or not a certain activity is 'ethical' or acceptable.

These are important questions, and ones I engage in regularly. However, there's more to philosophy than this. A typical discussion might, for example, begin by exploring whether illegally downloading films is unethical (it is) before moving to an exploration of how we think about responsibility, our attitudes towards art, and the influence of market consumerism. In this way, philosophy can help people look a little more closely at the practices and behaviours that define their lives. Sometimes this might reveal something we already know; at other times we might discover that our beliefs are hard to justify. Either way, merely by examining these ideas, we'll be doing something for the benefit of everyone.

31 How does the writer feel when he is asked about his job?

    A annoyed that people do not understand what he says

    B frustrated that people define themselves by their work

    C apprehensive about the reaction his response will cause

    D anxious to explain that he is no cleverer than anyone else

32 In the second paragraph, what does the writer say about human beings?

    A We all enjoy challenging the established cultural norms.

    B We are all capable of a certain degree of contemplation.

    C We are wary of those who stand in judgement of others.

    D We have lost the ability to learn from teachings of the past.

33 According to the third paragraph, an examined life is one in which a person

    A understands the practical application of their studies.

    B appreciates knowledge for its own sake.

    C considers their priorities.

    D lives apart from others.

34 The second reason the writer gives for the misconception about philosophers is that

    A few people ever find out about philosophical studies.

    B philosophers now work exclusively in universities.

    C philosophy has become less popular as a course of study.

    D the subjects which philosophers choose to focus on are obscure.

35 What does the writer say about the term 'ethicist' in the sixth paragraph?

    A He uses it to show he represents a new branch of philosophy.

    B The way in which it is used by philosophers has changed.

    C It makes clear his connection with the justice system.

    D It is too narrow to describe the work he does.

36 The writer uses the example of downloading films to show

    A the type of conversation that he thinks people should be having about philosophy.

    B how applied ethics can lead to considerations of more universal issues.

    C that the study of philosophy should play a greater role in modern life.

    D how people are able to ignore their own ethical failings.

Part 6

You are going to read four extracts from articles in which experts discuss Antarctica. For questions **37–40**, choose from the reviewers **A–D**. The reviewers may be chosen more than once.
Mark your answers **on the separate answer sheet**.

Antarctica

A Antarctica is a pristine and unspoilt continent. Not only is it unrivalled in its beauty but Antarctic science has revealed much about the impact of human activity on the natural world. For example, the discovery by scientists of the hole in the ozone layer above Antarctica revealed the damage done to the Earth's atmosphere by man-made chemicals. The fact that Antarctica is so vital for such scientific knowledge, to my mind, suggests that it must be left undisturbed in order to allow further scientific research on such critical international issues as climate change, long-range weather forecasting and the operation of marine eco-systems (crucial to sustainable fishing). If mines to exploit its natural resources were to be placed on the continent, these would undoubtedly affect the scientific readings. Only by having Antarctica completely untouched can we guarantee the level of accuracy we now have.

B Access to Antarctica should be restricted to those with a serious purpose. To suggest an example, almost 30,000 tourists are expected this year in what is, to my mind, a place of unparalleled charm in the universe. Most of them will be on cruise ships, which call at Antarctica's sites for just a few days. This number is, however, rising rapidly and some visitors are now undertaking adventurous activities such as ski-hiking, scuba-diving, snowboarding and mountaineering. Unchecked, this influx of people is greatly increasing the problems of waste management and their activities are having a negative impact on the coastal environment and its wildlife. Adventure tourists also need to be rescued by the authorities from time to time, diverting resources from science. The more vessels visiting the continent, the greater the chance of catastrophic oil spills or for rogue operators to neglect their environmental responsibilities.

C There may come a time when the need for resources calls into question the need for Antarctica to be left alone. However, continuing systematic investigation in Antarctica must, under no circumstances, be allowed to come to an end. Antarctica is a large continent, so it seems possible that mining for its resources could occur on one side of the continent, while the other could be maintained for investigative purposes. The distances between the bases would ensure there would be no adverse effect on either area of work. Furthermore, as the scientists worked, they would be able to notice any abnormalities caused by the exploitation of resources. If any were to come to light, scientists could promote discussions with governments and mining companies in order to address the issues involved. In this way, scientists would ensure that any negative impact on this most enchanting of environments would be kept to a minimum, thus eliminating cause for concern.

D The vast continent of Antarctica has been a major focus of scientific exploration for relatively few decades when compared to most areas on Planet Earth. Despite its remoteness, it has always attracted visitors, whether for adventure or leisure purposes. However, let's not lose sight of the fact that it's just one region and there are undoubtedly others which are equally stunning. Antarctica should be for all of humanity, not just for elite scientists who seek to deny others the right to go there while simultaneously demanding huge sums of money for their research projects. If the continent were opened up to tourism, revenues from this could be taxed as a way of offsetting the cost of scientific research. In order to prevent resulting damage to the environment, the International Association of Antarctica Tour Operators operates a strict code of practice. Therefore, I see no reason why we should be unduly alarmed about adverse effects on the landscape in Antarctica.

Which expert

shares an opinion with A on the value of carrying out scientific research in Antarctica?	37
has a different opinion to D on restrictions on visitors to Antarctica?	38
holds a different view from the other three on the subject of the beauty of Antarctica?	39
expresses a similar view to C regarding harm to Antarctica?	40

Part 7

You are going to read an article about the difficulties of being an environmentalist. Six paragraphs have been removed from the article. Choose from the paragraphs **A–G** the one which fits each gap (**41–46**). There is one extra paragraph which you do not need to use.

Mark your answers **on the separate answer sheet**.

The unbearable hypocrisy of being an environmentalist

Canadian environmentalist Rosa Sharp explores the contradictions
inherent in the lives of those who choose to live a greener life

I consider myself an environmentalist, yet last weekend I spent five hours in a car dealership going through the rigmarole of getting a new car – arguably one of the most polluting devices in modern-day life.

41

In a similar vein, an environmental lawyer I know, who came to his profession amid a deep affinity for and desire to protect the environment, now works seventy hours a week in a city centre office, staring at his computer screen. The work in which he makes great strides to protect the natural world also prevents him from enjoying it, leaving him torn between the change he wants to create, and his ability to enjoy the countryside for more than the odd weekend between cases.

42

This unbearable hypocrisy is a struggle for the individual and a delight for the critic, yet it seems both necessary and inescapable. All of us exist within the very system we hope to change. I use a laptop, a smartphone, internet, electricity. Most of the publications I write anti-consumerism articles for are paid for by advertisements for consumer products. This delicate balancing act epitomises the seemingly inescapable reality of the modern world which we've built and which now runs our lives.

43

However, an escape of this kind also means losing priceless human connection and culture, as well as the chance to educate or inspire change in others.

The fear of navigating this intellectual conflict, as well as the fear of armchair critics declaring that you've failed is, I believe, at the heart of many people's reluctance to adopt more green practices.

44

Apparently, a decision to live in a way which limits the damage you're causing to the environment means instantly opening yourself up to harsh criticism. You never committed to changing everything in your life, and yet, having made one or two changes, you're suddenly expected to be able to justify just about any aspect of your life that your attacker chooses.

45

My own reluctant decision to continue running a car came about as a result of several carefully considered factors including the limited public transportation options in my city and six months of harsh Canadian winter. Yes it makes me feel bad, but choosing to try to be green means putting up with the fact that you'll fail, at least some of the time.

46

I think environmentalist George Monbiot sums it up best: 'Hypocrisy is the gap between your aspirations and your actions. Environmentalists have high aspirations – they want to live more ethically – and they will always fall short. But the alternative to hypocrisy isn't moral purity (no one manages that), but cynicism. Give me hypocrisy any day.'

A After all, most of us would be put off to discover that, by deciding to start cycling to work or buying only locally produced food, we have tacitly branded ourselves and joined the often-mocked world of righteously indignant environmentalists who protest against energy companies while still availing themselves of heated homes and gas-powered transportation.

B It seems cruel that trying to safeguard what you love should mean you are unable to experience it first-hand. But such contrasts exist in the lives of most environmentalists. Some of us own cars; some still eat meat. The more famous regularly fly great distances to speak about the horrific impact of carbon emissions – such as that released by the airplanes they arrived on.

C And after all, why should anyone have to do this? There's an assumption that you'll have all the answers. 'Why bother recycling when you still drive?' 'Aren't those annual flights erasing the impact of anything else you do?' Well, of course in an ideal world, we environmentalists would live completely ethically, but this isn't an ideal world.

D Although I advocate buying second-hand, I chose to lease new. I encourage walking, cycling and public transportation, and I do take advantage of these options regularly, yet here I was, accepting the keys and setting off with a shiny new ride and a sinking sense of discomfort.

E They provide a perfect illustration of how being an environmentalist has always been about the need to make compromises. For most of us, leaving modern life behind just isn't an option. However, the fact that living a greener existence is challenging doesn't mean we shouldn't do what we can.

F In order to avoid it, one would need to go off the grid; abandon modern living for a hut in the woods. It's a move which, if you're brave enough to make it, enables you to subtract most of your environmental impact, and I think everyone, myself included, fantasises about it from time to time.

G And I've come to realise that it's a compromise I can live with. We can either accept the *status quo*, or work towards something better. Doing so often looks less like an off-grid hut in the woods and more like finding a way to exist in an uncomfortably unsustainable society whilst also trying to change it.

Part 8

You are going to read an article about an artist who made a film which shows her daughter Billie between the ages of eleven and eighteen. For questions **47–56**, choose from the sections (**A–D**). The sections may be chosen more than once.

Mark your answers **on the separate answer sheet**.

Which section mentions

speculation as to the motives behind the project?	47
praise for the choice of medium used?	48
a difference in attitudes towards the project?	49
a recollection which remains very vivid?	50
details about personal habits which have remained constant?	51
something which the artist wishes to retain?	52
an assertion that the film contains a narrative element?	53
details of how content to be included was approved?	54
a reference to Billie's increased reluctance to reveal true feelings?	55
factors which made Billie feel limited by the project?	56

Growing up on film

A When artist and film maker Melanie Manchot's daughter Billie was 11, Manchot had the idea of videoing her for just one minute every month until she turned 18. And when she proposed the idea to her daughter, the answer was an instant affirmative as Billie was familiar with the processes involved. 'She grasped the idea quickly,' Manchot says. 'To me, it was a commitment from the beginning. I wanted it to last for seven years. For Billie, it was much lighter – a "let's try it".' Starting as Billie began her last term of primary school, the project slipped seamlessly into their routine. 'It was always at the beginning of the month, Billie back from school, at the end of my working day,' says Manchot. 'We'd go downstairs into the studio. I marked the spot where Billie would stand and where the camera would be and it stayed the same for seven years.'

B How does Billie remember the process? She thought that overall it was not that bad though there were times when she was less keen. She says: 'You have to stay in the one spot and there's no sound, so you can't really do much. I think the fact that it was a film, not photos, made it more representative. You can pose for a quick photo but when you're standing there for a minute, it feels more like you. It wasn't digital, so I didn't really see it afterwards. We might film for a year and then it would be sent off to be developed. I didn't have a sense of what it would all be like.' Manchot was equally uncertain: 'I didn't see it for long periods and didn't know what it would become. Billie had veto rights all the way through. She could always tell me that she wanted something to stay private. Then that piece of film would become a portrait for us as a family.'

C Filming for the project finished as Billie turned 18. Shortly afterwards, Manchot was invited to exhibit it. It was as if the whole thing had been planned – the exhibition started five days before Billie was due to go away to university. 'I was looking back at all this film, seeing the years gone by, putting it into a sequence – and Billie was packing up her whole life, ready to leave,' recalls Manchot. The installation, *11/18*, is an 18-minute sequence, with a screen for each year. 'There's no story,' says Manchot. 'But in a way, there is. It's the story of growing up.' Billie at 11 looks more playful, more relaxed. She laughs and yawns and shows things to the camera. The older Billie is more still, more wary, more steady and composed. There's the sense of an interior, a holding back. But still there's continuity. Certain gestures – the way she pushes back her hair and looks up, for example – survive from 11 into adulthood. In the final minute, all the images appear at the same time – all the Billies are present together. And then they are gone.

D What's striking for a parent is how fast we can forget our children's younger selves, how completely they vanish. Has making *11/18* helped Manchot hold on to every age and stage? 'When I see young children now, it seems such a distance,' she says. 'I remember Billie being six clearly and poignantly – we spent a month in Ibiza and I can almost project myself back to that time and see her and feel her, the size, the dimensions. But there are lots of times between that have disappeared because that's what time does – you can't hold on to it. I remember filming Billie so well – some of those memories are so powerful, what she wore, how she rolled up her T-shirt. The marks of where we had to stand are still there on the studio floor and I'm going to keep them there for ever. Maybe part of making this was to allow me as a mother and as an artist to stay more in touch with the many small moments that slip away.'

WRITING (1 hour 30 minutes)

Part 1

You **must** answer this question. Write your answer in **220–260** words in an appropriate style **on the separate answer sheet**.

---

1   Your class has just watched an online discussion about factors which influence our consumer choices. You have made the notes below:

> **Factors which influence our consumer choices:**
> * celebrities
> * peer pressure
> * marketing

> Some opinions expressed in the programme:
>
> "People want to be like their favourite stars."
>
> "No one wants to be different."
>
> "Who takes any notice of all those adverts?"

Write an essay for your tutor discussing **two** of the factors which influence our consumer choices in your notes. You should **explain which factor is more significant, giving reasons** to support your opinion.

You may, if you wish, make use of the opinions expressed in the programme, but you should use your own words as far as possible.

Part 2

Write an answer to **one** of the questions **2–4** in this part. Write your answer in **220–260** words in an appropriate style **on the separate answer sheet**. Put the question number in the box at the top of the page.

---

2   You were recently sent on a training course by the company you work for, and your manager has asked you to write a report on the training you received. In your report, you should briefly describe the training, explain why it was useful for your current job, and say how the new skills may help you in the future.

Write your **report**.

3   You receive an email from a friend.

> ...
>
> I hear you ran a half-marathon – that sounds interesting. What organisation were you raising money for? Why didn't you just give them some money?
>
> I look forward to hearing from you.

Write an email to your friend describing your experience, explaining the work of the organisation you were raising money for and saying whether you think such events are an effective way to support charities.

Write your **email**.

4   A car-sharing scheme has been running in your area for six months. You decide to write a review of the scheme for an English-language magazine. You should briefly explain how the scheme works in your area, and evaluate the advantages and disadvantages of such schemes, in general.

Write your **review**.

LISTENING (approximately 40 minutes)

Part 1

You will hear three different extracts. For questions **1–6**, choose the answer (**A**, **B** or **C**) which fits best according to what you hear. There are two questions for each extract.

Extract One

You hear two newspaper journalists talking about their work to a group of students.

1 The man gives the example of social media sites to

  A clarify how important they are in everyday life.

  B compare their usefulness with that of newspapers.

  C defend people's attitude to news nowadays.

2 What do they both think about their job?

  A It can be stressful at times.

  B It is important to be a team player.

  C There are more negatives than positives.

Extract Two

You hear two language teachers discussing the use of emoticons, the pictures many people use to express emotion in text messages.

3 What is the woman doing?

  A questioning the value of current research into emoticons

  B proposing ideas for potential uses of emoticons

  C identifying reasons for the popularity of emoticons

4 What do they both think about emoticons?

  A They need to be used with caution.

  B They are a lazy form of communication.

  C They have universal appeal.

Extract Three

You hear two friends talking about a young professional tennis player.

5   The woman feels that the comments about the player in the media reflect

   A   how easy it is to take sport too seriously.

   B   a common misconception about sportspeople.

   C   a lack of understanding amongst sports journalists.

6   How does the man feel about the player's outbursts of anger?

   A   It's essential that they're kept in check.

   B   They're understandable in the circumstances.

   C   He's irritated about the way they'll be perceived.

Part 2

You will hear a woman called Jane Brooks talking about her work on various marine conservation projects. For questions **7–14**, complete the sentences with a word or short phrase.

Conservation work

When choosing her first volunteer job, Jane was undecided between marine conservation in

Thailand and a **(7)** .... scheme in Belize.

In Cambodia, Jane is employed as a **(8)** .... working with volunteers.

Jane went from diving at intermediate level to receiving her official

(9) .... in under six months.

Jane contrasts her present situation, living in the centre of a **(10)** .... ,

with her time in Thailand.

Jane uses the expression **(11)** .... to describe the way the local people

view her.

Something that Jane finds particularly upsetting is the number of

(12) .... that the volunteers recover from the sea.

As part of her current project's wider aims, Jane says they will be helping set up a

(13) .... scheme.

One of the things Jane enjoys most is watching new divers gain

(14) .... during the learning process.

Part 3

You will hear an interview with two college lecturers, Sarah Banks and Tom Weston, who are talking about working in clothes shops when they were students. For questions **15–20**, choose the answer (**A**, **B**, **C** or **D**) which fits best according to what you hear.

15 Regarding her choice of job in an expensive clothes store, Sarah
    A wanted to develop her retail skills.
    B accepted it because of a lack of alternatives.
    C felt it would suit her interest in high-end fashion.
    D hoped to meet influential clients.

16 Sarah says one aspect of the job she enjoyed was
    A selecting the perfect clothes for demanding clients.
    B creating an atmosphere in which clients felt comfortable.
    C seeing how certain clothes could transform clients' appearance.
    D observing how clients would often make inappropriate choices.

17 What was Sarah's approach to the staff dress code?
    A She admits she turned her choice of clothes into a kind of protest.
    B She took the opportunity to break the rules whenever possible.
    C She was proud to wear the shop's clothes outside her workplace.
    D She found it relatively easy to conform to what was required.

18 How did Tom feel about what he overheard while working in a boutique?
    A sad that his suspicions about his boss were confirmed
    B disappointed that colleagues had concealed things from him
    C frustrated that his ideas were so readily rejected
    D infuriated with himself for having been so naïve

19 In Tom's opinion, the students he teaches who have had work experience are
    A less likely to require help in order to cope with academic life.
    B inclined to take a healthy financial situation for granted.
    C prepared to make sacrifices for the sake of their studies.
    D more critical about the quality of the courses they're following.

20 What do Sarah and Tom agree that they learnt from their work experience as students?
    A People tend to behave in the same way wherever they shop.
    B Retail skills can be applied in a range of other contexts.
    C Shop work presents a unique chance to develop people skills.
    D Any kind of job can bring an improvement in self-esteem.

Part 4

You will hear five short extracts in which people are talking about their favourite series of travel guidebooks.

TASK ONE

For questions **21–25**, choose from the list (**A–H**) what each speaker particularly likes about the series of travel guidebooks.

TASK TWO

For questions **26–30**, choose from the list (**A–H**) one criticism each speaker has of the series of travel guidebooks.

While you listen, you must complete both tasks.

A	the coverage of cultural aspects	**A** unnecessary information
B	their organisation into ready-made tour schedules	**B** focus on popular destinations
C	their value as background research	**C** lack of practical detail
D	the variety of the images	**D** confusing visuals
E	the contributions from respected authors	**E** lack of expressive language in parts
F	the enjoyable style of writing	**F** inconvenient to carry
G	the environmentally-friendly format	**G** old-fashioned feel
H	the linguistic support offered	**H** out-of-date content

TASK ONE

Speaker 1		21
Speaker 2		22
Speaker 3		23
Speaker 4		24
Speaker 5		25

TASK TWO

Speaker 1		26
Speaker 2		27
Speaker 3		28
Speaker 4		29
Speaker 5		30

SPEAKING (15 minutes)

There are two examiners. One (the interlocutor) conducts the test, providing you with the necessary materials and explaining what you have to do. The other examiner (the assessor) is introduced to you, but then takes no further part in the interaction.

Part 1 (2 minutes)

The interlocutor first asks you and your partner for some information about yourselves, then widens the scope of the questions by asking about e.g. your leisure activities, studies, travel and daily life. You are expected to respond to the interlocutor's questions and listen to what your partner has to say.

Part 2 (a one-minute 'long turn' for each candidate, plus a 30-second response from the second candidate)

You are each given the opportunity to talk for about a minute, and to comment briefly after your partner has spoken.

The interlocutor gives you a set of three pictures and asks you to talk about two of them for about one minute. It is important to listen carefully to the interlocutor's instructions. The interlocutor then asks your partner a question about your pictures and your partner responds briefly.

You are then given another set of pictures to look at. Your partner talks about these pictures for about one minute. This time the interlocutor asks you a question about your partner's pictures and you respond briefly.

Part 3 (4 minutes)

In this part of the test, you and your partner are asked to talk together. The interlocutor places a question and some text prompts on the table between you. This stimulus provides the basis for a discussion, after which you will need to make a decision on the topic in question. The interlocutor explains what you have to do.

Part 4 (5 minutes)

The interlocutor asks some further questions, which leads to a more general discussion of the topic you have discussed in Part 3. You may comment on your partner's answers if you wish.

Test 4

READING AND USE OF ENGLISH (1 hour 30 minutes)

Part 1

For questions **1–8**, read the text below and decide which answer (**A, B, C** or **D**) best fits each gap. There is an example at the beginning (**0**).
Mark your answers **on the separate answer sheet**.

Example:

0 A provision   **B** output   **C** yield   **D** supply

0	A	B	C	D
	▭	▬	▭	▭

A taste of the future

Experimental psychologists, who have influenced the **(0)** …….. of food industry giants by studying how our senses interact to form our perception of flavour, are turning their attention to the menus of leading restaurants. How to make bug-eating acceptable to westerners is just one of the problems they are **(1)** …….. .

Sensory testing has already been used to **(2)** …….. how consumers are affected by the colours in packaging. It was found that increasing the amount of yellow on cans of lemonade **(3)** …….. people they could taste more lemon. **(4)** …….. the researchers are also helping brands to produce healthier food by making reductions in the salt and sugar they contain. If this is done **(5)** …….. , customers don't notice the difference from one packet to the **(6)** …….. .

Their study of how we experience food has already provided some fascinating **(7)** …….. for chefs. The colour of crockery, the weight of cutlery, background noise – these all control taste, and people, not surprisingly perhaps, eat more when in the **(8)** …….. of friends.

1 **A** tackling   **B** grappling   **C** cracking   **D** managing

2 **A** dictate   **B** decide   **C** direct   **D** determine

3 **A** tricked   **B** convinced   **C** swayed   **D** influenced

4 **A** Lately   **B** Instantly   **C** Currently   **D** Shortly

5 **A** repeatedly   **B** cautiously   **C** regularly   **D** gradually

6 **A** next   **B** previous   **C** second   **D** following

7 **A** insights   **B** judgements   **C** features   **D** elements

8 **A** party   **B** crowd   **C** group   **D** company

Part 2

For questions **9–16**, read the text below and think of the word which best fits each gap. Use only **one** word in each gap. There is an example at the beginning (**0**).
Write your answers **IN CAPITAL LETTERS on the separate answer sheet**.

Example: | **0** | | T | H | E | | | | | | | | | | | | | | |

Safer cycling

Everyone is familiar with **(0)** …….. workings of airbags in cars, designed to absorb the impact of a crash. But now an airbag for cyclists has been invented and it's being promoted **(9)** …….. a helmet for people who don't like wearing helmets.

When I started cycling, I always wore a helmet but after many years without ever really needing its protection, I started to leave it behind – **(10)** …….. because of vanity, rather because of the hassle of having to carry it once I'd parked my bike.

The cyclist's airbag fits round your neck a bit **(11)** …….. a scarf. It's heavier than it looks, which I put down **(12)** …….. the fact that it includes a device that stops it being activated unnecessarily. In order to test it, I had to throw myself **(13)** …….. the bike, head first. In mid-air, moments **(14)** …….. I landed on the ground, I heard a loud bang. Then, **(15)** …….. I was, lying next to my bike, wrapped in a firm white balloon. It certainly worked well but I'm not sure if it's good value **(16)** …….. money as it can only be used once. Maybe I should go back to my helmet.

Part 3

For questions **17–24**, read the text below. Use the word given in capitals at the end of some of the lines to form a word that fits in the gap **in the same line**. There is an example at the beginning (**0**). Write your answers **IN CAPITAL LETTERS on the separate answer sheet**.

Example: | 0 | F | O | R | T | U | N | A | T | E | L | Y | | | | | | | |

Laughter

Laughter is the best medicine they say and (**0**) …….. it's contagious. **FORTUNE**

You know the situation – someone laughs and we (**17**) …….. laugh **MIND**

in turn, without knowing why we've joined in. It's a totally (**18**) …….. **VOLUNTARY**

response – just the sound of a laugh is enough to prompt it spreading.

It's no surprise, therefore, that recorded laughter is added to

television sitcoms. This laugh track (**19**) …….. the programme, in **COMPANY**

the absence of a live audience, to stimulate laughter among the

(**20**) …….. at home. **VIEW**

Naturally, the likelihood of our laughing is much greater in social

situations. Laughing with people brings the (**21**) …….. of feeling **PLEASE**

accepted by the group; the only thing we have to be careful of is not

to laugh (**22**) …….. as that would destroy the positive group feeling. **APPROPRIATE**

Laughter can be a particularly informative measure of relationships

because it's largely (**23**) …….. and hard to fake. As it's also a good **PLAN**

guide to people's innermost (**24**) …….. , learning how to 'read' these **THINK**

would be a valuable life skill.

Part 4

For questions **25–30**, complete the second sentence so that it has a similar meaning to the first sentence, using the word given. **Do not change the word given.** You must use between **three** and **six** words, including the word given. Here is an example (**0**).

Example:

0 James would only speak to the head of department alone.

ON

James .... to the head of department alone.

The gap can be filled with the words 'insisted on speaking', so you write:

Example:	0	INSISTED ON SPEAKING

Write **only** the missing words **IN CAPITAL LETTERS on the separate answer sheet.**

---

25   'I've never given this presentation before,' Mary admitted.

   FIRST

   Mary admitted that it was .... given that presentation.

26   Jane knew she should arrive at the airport two hours early.

   MEANT

   Jane knew she .... up at the airport two hours early.

27   Lisa was a good candidate so not surprisingly she was offered the job.

   CAME

   Lisa was a good candidate so it .... that she was offered the job.

28 Sally completely ignored the advice I gave her and bought that awful car.

NOTICE

Sally ………………………………….. the advice I gave her and bought that awful car.

29 The price of computers has come down over the last few years.

DROP

There ………………………………….. the price of computers over the last few years.

30 It'll be sunny later, so it's a good idea to apply some sunscreen.

BETTER

It'll be sunny later, so you ………………………………….. on some sunscreen.

Part 5

You are going to read a magazine article about whether or not animals have emotions. For questions **31–36**, choose the answer (**A, B, C** or **D**) which you think fits best according to the text. Mark your answers **on the separate answer sheet**.

Animal Emotions

Tom Whipple asks 'Do animals really have emotions? And what are the consequences if they do?'

In a Swedish zoo a chimpanzee called Santino spent his nights breaking up concrete into pieces to throw at visitors during the day. Was he being spiteful? In caves in the US, female bats help unrelated fruit bat mothers if they can't find the right birthing position. Are they being caring? Fifty years ago, these questions would have been largely seen as irrelevant. Animals had behaviours, the behaviours produced measurable outcomes, and science recorded those outcomes. The idea that animals have consciousness, feelings and moral systems was sloppy and sentimental.

But recently that has partially changed. Thanks to research into the behaviour of bats, chimps, not to mention rats, dolphins and chickens, emotions of animals have gone from being a taboo area of investigation to being tentatively explored. It is a change that has in recent years filtered through the scientific strata to a selection of popular science books, such as Mark Bekoff's *Wild Justice* and Victoria Braithwaite's *Do Fish Feel Pain*? And in the process it has started a debate that may never be solved by science: can animals be said to have consciousness?

This debate stimulates a second, much less abstract, one: not of consciousness, but conscience – a person's moral sense of right and wrong that guides their behaviour. In a recent experiment involving cows that had to open a locked gate in order to get food, it became apparent that those that successfully opened the gate themselves showed more pleasure – by jumping and kicking their legs – than those that had to have the gate opened for them. If, as this research seems to imply, cows enjoy problem-solving, what does it mean for the production and consumption of beef?

The observations may not be disputed, but the interpretation of them is. According to Dr Jonathan Balcombe, author of *Second Nature*, the only logically consistent response to the new research is to stop eating meat. For him, humanity is on the verge of the greatest revolution in ethics since the abolition of slavery. According to Aubrey Manning, Professor Emeritus at Edinburgh University, we should at the very least re-evaluate our view of animal cognition. For him, 'the only tenable hypothesis is that animals do have a theory of mind, but it's simpler than ours.' And according to Professor Euan MacPhail we should just stop anthropomorphising. The three may never be reconciled because the crux of the issue is not so much a scientific disagreement, or even a moral one, but a philosophical one. Given that even defining consciousness is near impossible, can we ever hope to know, in the words of the philosopher Thomas Nagel, what it is like to be a bat? Let alone a bat midwife.

Balcombe describes a landmark experiment he did that – in his interpretation – appears to show that starlings – a type of bird – can get depressed. In a study at Newcastle University, starlings were split into two groups. Half were housed in luxurious cages, with plenty of space and water. The other half were housed in small, barren cages. Initially both groups were fed with tasty worms from one box and unpleasant worms from another, and soon learned to take only from the tasty box. But subsequently when the birds were offered only unpleasant worms, only the ones housed in luxurious cages would eat. It seemed, or at least Balcombe concluded, that being in a nasty cage caused the starlings to be pessimistic about life in general.

Balcombe, who has worked with animal rights groups, has a clear bias. 'We look back with abhorrence on an era where there was racism,' he says. 'Our view about animals will someday be the same. We can't espouse animal rights between bites of a cheeseburger.' If he were the only advocate of this view of animal consciousness, it might be easy to dismiss him as an extremist. Unfortunately for those who might prefer to ignore Balcombe, Professor Aubrey Manning is in the same camp. Manning has written a textbook, *An Introduction to Animal Behaviour*. 'What we are seeing is a pendulum swing,' he says. 'At the turn of the 20th century there were people who made assumptions that animals thought just like us, and there was a reaction against that. Now we are going the other way. But it is a highly contentious subject and you really want to try to avoid the sound of academics with various personal grievances and strong personal opinions.'

31 In the first paragraph the writer suggests that

    A   some older animal research would now be seen as unscientific.
    B   some animals respond too unpredictably to be included in reliable study data.
    C   some animal research has come to conclusions that are highly questionable.
    D   some animal behaviour is difficult to explain through a traditional approach.

32 In the second paragraph, what point is the writer making about the idea that animals have emotions?

    A   It has been confused by many with another issue.
    B   It has moved beyond mere academic speculation.
    C   It has been fully accepted by the scientific community.
    D   It has contradicted another recent proposal on the topic.

33 When the writer mentions cows, he is saying that

    A   scientists now believe that certain animals have a sense of morality.
    B   some animals are fundamentally unsuited to being kept in captivity.
    C   the question of how animals should be treated needs to be re-examined.
    D   the number of animals demonstrating intelligence is higher than previously thought.

34 In the fourth paragraph, what conclusion does the writer draw about the differing views of experts?

    A   Some of them verge on the ridiculous.
    B   They are based on flawed evidence.
    C   They do not warrant further investigation.
    D   A consensus is unlikely ever to be reached.

35 In the fifth paragraph, it is clear that the writer

    A   wishes to be seen as objectively reporting Balcombe's experiment.
    B   intends to defend Balcombe against a possible criticism.
    C   is questioning the details of Balcombe's methods.
    D   agrees in principle with Balcombe's ideas.

36 What is said in the final paragraph about Balcombe's views?

    A   They have been directly influenced by research from a previous era.
    B   They are shared by an eminent authority on the subject.
    C   They have been rejected as extreme by one opponent.
    D   They are seen as objectionable in some quarters.

Part 6

You are going to read four extracts from articles in which sports experts discuss hosting the Olympic Games. For questions **37–40**, choose from the experts **A–D**. The experts may be chosen more than once.

Mark your answers **on the separate answer sheet**.

Is hosting the Olympic Games worthwhile?

Four sports experts look at the pros and cons of hosting the summer Olympic Games

A It's clear that, both just before and immediately after the Olympics, the number of people routinely doing physical activity rises in the host country. But the main reason cities bid to hold the Olympics is that, perhaps against the odds, it's wildly popular with the voters who foot the bill. I say 'against the odds' because there is strikingly little evidence to suggest that such events draw new investment. Spending lavishly on a short-lived event is, financially speaking, a dubious long-term strategy. Additionally, when a city hosts the Olympics, those who may have been considering visiting it turn to other destinations in order to avoid the crowds. I don't think the issue would be solved by spreading the Games over more than one city, as this wouldn't be popular. In Sydney, for example, as many sports as possible were crammed into a dedicated Olympic Park, and the concept was very well received.

B It's rarely the case that all Olympic events are held in a single city. Early-round soccer games, for example, take place in many different towns. Still, hosting the Olympics poses a high risk to the leaders of the city involved. While in some places initial negativity turns to more positive emotions once the Games begin, in others strong local support during the bidding process can sour as the level of spending necessary becomes clear. Such a change seems rather unjust to me as cities which host the Olympics clearly experience a significant increase in trade. The positive impact on numbers of travellers including the host city in their itinerary is also generally quite significant. On the other hand, my research shows no direct link between the profile and popularity of a sport at the elite level during the Olympics and its subsequent uptake at the grassroots level in host cities.

C I think it's significant that, in the most recent round of bidding to host the Olympics, several world-famous cities withdrew after failing to summon sufficient support among their own citizens. Their objections were almost exclusively based around the huge budgets involved. Supporters like to point to the commerce that the Olympics has supposedly brought to certain cities. But that commerce was going to spring up anyway. It was not directly connected to the Olympics. The Olympics have become too big and expensive to have in one place. In this age of instant communication, there's simply no need to condense the Games in one overburdened location. Better distribution would also spread the associated rise in demand for hotels and restaurants that is one noticeable benefit of hosting the Games. Another is the increase in the number of people who, for example, join teams or start running regularly following the Olympics. We see this in almost all host cities.

D Every time we've analysed it, the conclusion has been the same: there is no real monetary benefit in hosting the Olympic Games. Temporary surges in consumer spending associated with a spike in arrivals from overseas may help to offset the expense of hosting, but it's clear that hosting the Olympics has become a burden. The solution, however, is simple – choose a range of cities to host, not just one. Politicians bid for the Olympics hoping it will increase their popularity. However, even if the bid is successful, the politicians involved are seldom still around once the event starts seven years later. And as for the claim that hosting the Games leads to fitter citizens, well we only have to look at London. Since the Olympics there, the number of people taking exercise for a minimum of thirty minutes at least once a week has actually declined.

Which expert

expresses a different view from the other three regarding the effect that hosting the Olympics has on the economy of the host city?

| 37 | |

has a different opinion from B on whether hosting the Olympics increases tourism in the host city?

| 38 | |

shares an opinion with B about whether hosting the Olympics increases participation in sport among residents of the host city?

| 39 | |

shares an opinion with C regarding the idea that several cities should get together to host the Olympic Games?

| 40 | |

Part 7

You are going to read a newspaper article about editing the sound in movies. Six paragraphs have been removed from the article. Choose from the paragraphs **A–G** the one which fits each gap (**41–46**). There is one extra paragraph which you do not need to use.

Mark your answers **on the separate answer sheet**.

The art of sound in movies

The monstrous complexity of sound editing work – the quest to make films sound the way the world sounds – may not be immediately apparent. After a movie has been filmed, it enters the labyrinthine world of post-production, in which the best takes are selected and spliced together into roughly 20-minute segments of film. These are worked on and then stitched together at the end of post-production.

41

The distinction between these processes is subtle: the first two have more to do with the creation and selection of the sounds that make up each scene, and the development of a cohesive aural aesthetic for a movie. The third involves taking sounds created by the designers and editors and integrating them in each scene so that everything comes across as 'natural'.

42

First, editors remove the audio recordings taken during filming and break down each scene into distinct sonic elements, namely dialogue, effects, music and Foley. 'Foley' is the term used for everyday sounds such as squeaky shoes or cutlery jangling in a drawer.

43

Consider a classic movie scene in which something important has just happened, for example a villain has just pulled up in his car. There are a few moments of what might be mistaken for stillness. Nothing moves – but the soundscape is deceptively layered There might be a mostly unnoticeable rustle of leaves in the trees periodically, so faint that almost no one would register it consciously. Or the sound of a vehicle rolling through an intersection a block or two over; off camera, a dog barks somewhere far away.

44

All this requires a very particular and somewhat strange set of talents and fascinations. You need the ability not only to hear with an almost superhuman ear, but also the technical proficiency and saint-like patience to spend hours getting the sound of a kettle's hiss exactly the right length as well as the right pitch – and not only the right pitch but the right pitch considering that the camera moves across the scene during the shot.

45

This is why there is something very slightly unnerving about spending time around people whose powers of perception suggest the existence of an entirely different layer of reality that you are missing. The way they work requires an entirely different – and, in some senses, unnatural – way of experiencing sound. The process reflects the fact that each sound is important enough to deserve its own consideration, so each gets edited separately before being put all together and checked for coherence.

46

Consequently, the vast majority of people walk around not hearing most of what there is to hear. Not so, for most sound editors. It can be mildly excruciating to listen this hard, to hear so much, which is why some of the team wear earplugs when they walk around the city.

A Each of these components needs to be built and then edited separately for every scene before being assigned its own dedicated editor. Then, the top guys take the team's work and layer it to make scenes that sound like the real world sounds.

B The gesture had the studious flourish which a minor orchestral instrumentalist – say, the triangle player – might devote to his one entrance. But instead of being the work of the actor, likely as not, that was a moustachioed man standing in his socks in a warehouse somewhere.

C This is radically unlike the way the human brain is designed to hear. We are predisposed to heed the rhythms and pitch of people talking and noises that might indicate threat. Other sounds – like 'white noise' – are depressed so that the brain fires fewer responses and we automatically 'tune out'. This is how the brain converts sound into information.

D The viewer's ear will subconsciously anticipate hearing a maddeningly subtle, but critical, Doppler effect, which means that the tone it makes as it boils needs to shift downward at precisely the interval that a real one would if you happened to walk by at that speed.

E Each part goes through picture editing (for such things as visual continuity or colour) before being handed over to the sound supervisor, who oversees all the various elements of sound design, sound editing, and mixing.

F When the thud of his boot heel finally connects with the asphalt, his breathing is laboured, even the pads of his fingers creak as they make contact with the collar of his leather jacket as he straightens. None of these are there because some microphone picked them up. They're there because someone chose them and put them there, like every other sound in the film.

G In other words, it is important to make sure the sound of a butterfly landing on the hood of a car isn't louder than a car backfiring. Only a few people have an ear for these types of work.

Part 8

You are going to read an article in which a scientist discusses the mistaken ideas people have about his profession. For questions **47–56**, choose from the sections (**A–D**). The sections may be chosen more than once.

Mark your answers **on the separate answer sheet**.

In which section does the writer

speculate about the experiences of other professionals?	47
suggest motives for the actions of particular scientists?	48
explain why an individual cannot be familiar with all branches of science?	49
suggest that being famous can cause people to behave in a particular way?	50
admit that a common portrayal of scientists achieves its purpose?	51
use an example from another profession to support an observation about human nature?	52
admit to a personal bias?	53
mention the role of the team in the advancement of scientific knowledge?	54
admit to a minor wrongdoing?	55
mention that misunderstandings about science are rooted in curriculum design?	56

Why people think scientists know everything

Neuroscientist Dean Burnett considers the reasons why people often have the wrong idea about science and scientists.

A One unexpected aspect of being a scientist is the weird questions you get asked by non-scientists. Whilst publicising my latest book, I've been asked many. Among my favourites is: 'Which are smarter, tigers or wolves?' As a neuroscientist, I'm not trained to answer this (assuming an answer even exists). Obviously, if I'm going to put myself out there as an authority on things, then I should expect questions. However, this happened to me even before I became a public figure, and other scientists I've spoken to report similar, regular occurrences. It's just something people do, like meeting a doctor at a party and asking them about a rash. If you're a scientist, people assume you know all science, something which would require several lifetimes of study. In truth, most scientists are, just like experts in any other field, very specialist. If you meet a historian who specialises in 19th-century Britain, asking them about ancient Egyptians is illogical. Maybe this does happen to historians. I can't say. It happens to scientists though. So where does this 'scientists know all science' preconception come from?

B Because my area of interest is the human brain, I tend to blame it for many of life's problems. For example, the way in which it handles information could lead to this idea of the all-knowing scientist. Our brain has to deal with a lot of information, so it often uses short cuts. One of these is to clump information together. While functionally useful, you can see how this would lead to inaccuracies or even prejudices. If someone struggles to understand science, in their heads it all gets lumped together as 'stuff I don't understand'. The same goes for scientists, who may get labelled as 'people who understand things I don't'. Education also plays a role. The study of science gets more specific the further you progress, but at a young age you get taught what's called simply 'science'. So you begin with this notion that science is just one subject, and have to gradually figure out otherwise. Would it be surprising then, if many people never really move on from this perception due to a disinterest in science, and consequently continue to regard scientists as interchangeable?

C The way in which scientists are portrayed in the media doesn't help either. Any new discovery or development reported in the press invariably begins with 'Scientists have discovered...' or 'According to scientists...'. You seldom get this in any other field. The latest government initiative does not begin with 'Politicians have decided...'. If any study or finding worth mentioning is invariably attributed to all scientists everywhere, it's understandable if the average reader ends up thinking they're all one and the same. The press also love the idea of the 'lone genius'. The story of a scientific discovery typically focuses on a single, brilliant intellectual, changing the world via his or her all-encompassing genius. While this makes for an inspiring narrative and therefore sells newspapers, it's far from the collaborative effort which most science is the result of. In fiction too, we constantly encounter the stand-alone genius who knows everything about everything, usually in very helpful and plot-relevant ways. This is bound to rub off on some people in the real world.

D Of course, this whole thing would be easier if it weren't for actual scientists making matters worse. Some, maybe unintentionally, make declarations about other fields which don't agree with what the evidence says. I've even done it myself occasionally. In popular science books, it's not uncommon for the author to stray into areas that they aren't that familiar with but which need to be addressed in order to provide a coherent argument. Sadly, you also get the scientists who, having achieved influence and prestige, start to believe their own press and end up making declarations about fields beyond their own, using confidence instead of actual awareness of how things work. Because such people have a public platform, the public assumes they must be right. The fact is that if scientists really did know everything, they'd know how to put an end to the misconceptions about their professions. But they don't. So they don't.

WRITING (1 hour 30 minutes)

Part 1

You **must** answer this question. Write your answer in **220–260** words in an appropriate style on **the separate answer sheet**.

---

1   Your class has just watched a TV documentary on factors influencing social trends. You have made the notes below:

Factors influencing social trends:
- communications
- opportunities
- advertising

Some opinions expressed in the discussion:

"The smartphone has transformed social interaction."

"Education and travel can affect people's tastes."

"No one can escape the social pressures of advertising."

Write an essay for your tutor discussing **two** of the factors in your notes. You should **explain which factor you think has greater influence on social trends, giving reasons** to support your opinion.

You may, if you wish, make use of the opinions expressed in the discussion, but you should use your own words as far as possible.

Part 2

Write an answer to **one** of the questions **2–4** in this part. Write your answer in **220–260** words in an appropriate style **on the separate answer sheet**. Put the question number in the box at the top of the page.

---

2   Local businesses have set up a fund to pay for a community facility in the area where you live, for example, a theatre, a nature reserve or perhaps an ice rink. The organisers have asked residents to give their opinions about how the fund should be used. You decide to write a proposal suggesting a facility, justifying your choice and explaining why you think it would be beneficial for the community.

Write your **proposal**.

3   You receive this email from an English-speaking friend:

> …
>
> I'm about to start a business course at college and I'm wondering whether it'd be a good idea to take on a part-time job at the same time – I know that's what you did. How difficult did you find it to balance your work and study time? Can you suggest the most suitable kind of job to look for? I'd be grateful for any ideas and suggestions.

Write your **email**.

4   An international college magazine has asked for reviews of television documentaries. You decide to write a review of a documentary you have seen on learning languages.

Your review should explain what you found out about different ways of learning languages and evaluate how interesting the documentary was.

Write your **review**.

LISTENING (approximately 40 minutes)

Part 1

You will hear three different extracts. For questions **1–6**, choose the answer (**A**, **B** or **C**) which fits best according to what you hear. There are two questions for each extract.

Extract One

You hear two friends talking about their children's reading habits.

1   The man says his daughter is motivated to read when

    A she is attracted by a book's illustrations.

    B she is allowed to choose which books to read.

    C she is able to identify with the characters in books.

2   They both feel that children who don't read for pleasure

    A tend to associate books with studying.

    B have too many other leisure distractions.

    C are following the pattern set by parents.

Extract Two

You hear part of an interview with a man who worked as a team leader with students doing voluntary work in the rainforest.

3   When talking about the volunteers, he reveals that he is

    A admiring of how quickly they adapted to a new environment.

    B proud of the way they developed as people whilst there.

    C appreciative of their efforts to complete the project on time.

4   What does he feel he gained most from the experience of being a team leader?

    A a stronger sense of his own potential

    B the ability to deal with the unexpected

    C greater understanding of how people behave in groups

Extract Three

You hear two students talking about fast food.

5   The man says his housemates choose to eat fast food because

    A they've been influenced by marketing campaigns.

    B the generous size of servings represents good value.

    C their lack of cooking skills makes it an attractive option.

6   What is the woman's attitude to fast food?

    A She criticises its unappetising flavours.

    B She welcomes the new options available.

    C She doubts whether improved labelling will affect its popularity.

Part 2

You will hear an architectural photographer called Jack Gollins talking about his work immediately after receiving a professional award. For questions **7–14**, complete the sentences with a word or short phrase.

Architectural photographer

Jack says it was a conversation with **(7)** .... that made him

aware of how much work he's done during his career.

One of Jack's personal rules is that, unlike other architectural photographers, he shoots

photos with a **(8)** .... lens.

Jack uses the expression **(9)** .... to refer to places containing

buildings that have had a strong impact on him.

Jack recalls the need for powerful **(10)** .... when working in India.

Jack refers to his visits overseas as **(11)** .... for developing his

professional skills.

Jack explains how collaborating with a particular **(12)** .... has

helped him take elevated shots.

By doing a number of fast **(13)** .... , Jack is able to shoot from

the sky without annoying people on the ground.

Jack explains that capturing what he calls the **(14)** .... can be

very important financially.

Part 3

You will hear part of an interview in which a science writer called Andy Hicks and a psychologist called Dr Karen Ferrigan are talking about how technology affects our brains. For questions **15–20**, choose the answer (**A**, **B**, **C** or **D**) which fits best according to what you hear.

15 What point does Andy make about multitasking?
    A   Few people have the ability to master it effectively.
    B   People fail to understand its implications for their lifestyle.
    C   The different interpretations of what it means are valid.
    D   The idea itself is a popular misconception.

16 When asked about the effect of unread emails on intelligence, Andy says
    A   it is purely temporary in nature.
    B   it suggests people are easily able to change focus.
    C   it has been over-simplified by researchers.
    D   it is less dramatic than previously supposed.

17 Andy mentions workplace studies in order to illustrate
    A   the advantages of letting people multitask.
    B   how common self-deception is.
    C   a personal experience he has had.
    D   the need for more directed research.

18 Karen feels that problems with remembering passwords are due to
    A   the way the brain organises data.
    B   issues with different types of memory.
    C   inconsistent rules that users have to follow.
    D   the information overload now imposed on people.

19 What does Karen see as a key issue with the human brain?
    A   the methods used to do research into its workings
    B   how it struggles to keep up with technological change
    C   the way it physically adapts to environmental changes
    D   how bad it is at making effective decisions

20 When asked about the benefits of the information age, Karen and Andy disagree about
    A   the accuracy of the information we can access.
    B   the risks of neglecting traditional sources of information.
    C   the effects on people's abilities to retain information.
    D   the priorities for helping people exploit the mass of information available.

Part 4

You will hear five short extracts in which people are talking about their experiences of doing volunteer work.

TASK ONE

For questions **21–25**, choose from the list **(A–H)** the reason each speaker gives for doing volunteer work.

TASK TWO

For questions **26–30**, choose from the list **(A–H)** the change each speaker identifies in themselves as a result of doing volunteer work.

While you listen, you must complete both tasks.

A to overcome a fear	**A** better time management
B to meet like-minded people	**B** an ability to deal with difficult people
C to acquire practical skills	**C** enhanced powers of concentration
D to clarify future options	**D** an appreciation of family
E to make a significant impact	**E** improved level of fitness
F to match friends' expectations	**F** an understanding of ecological problems
G to fill time usefully	**G** a stronger sense of indentity
H to learn about the natural world	**H** a greater awareness of others

Speaker 1	21		Speaker 1	26
Speaker 2	22		Speaker 2	27
Speaker 3	23		Speaker 3	28
Speaker 4	24		Speaker 4	29
Speaker 5	25		Speaker 5	30

SPEAKING (15 minutes)

There are two examiners. One (the interlocutor) conducts the test, providing you with the necessary materials and explaining what you have to do. The other examiner (the assessor) is introduced to you, but then takes no further part in the interaction.

Part 1 (2 minutes)

The interlocutor first asks you and your partner for some information about yourselves, then widens the scope of the questions by asking about e.g. your leisure activities, studies, travel and daily life. You are expected to respond to the interlocutor's questions and listen to what your partner has to say.

Part 2 (a one-minute 'long turn' for each candidate, plus a 30-second response from the second candidate)

You are each given the opportunity to talk for about a minute, and to comment briefly after your partner has spoken.

The interlocutor gives you a set of three pictures and asks you to talk about two of them for about one minute. It is important to listen carefully to the interlocutor's instructions. The interlocutor then asks your partner a question about your pictures and your partner responds briefly.

You are then given another set of pictures to look at. Your partner talks about these pictures for about one minute. This time the interlocutor asks you a question about your partner's pictures and you respond briefly.

Part 3 (4 minutes)

In this part of the test, you and your partner are asked to talk together. The interlocutor places a question and some text prompts on the table between you. This stimulus provides the basis for a discussion, after which you will need to make a decision on the topic in question.
The interlocutor explains what you have to do.

Part 4 (5 minutes)

The interlocutor asks some further questions, which leads to a more general discussion of the topic you have discussed in Part 3. You may comment on your partner's answers if you wish.

CAMBRIDGE ENGLISH
Language Assessment
Part of the University of Cambridge

Do not write in this box

SAMPLE

Candidate Name
If not already printed, write name in CAPITALS and complete the Candidate No. grid (in pencil).

Candidate Signature

Examination Title

Centre

Supervisor:
If the candidate is ABSENT or has WITHDRAWN shade here

Centre No.

Candidate No.

Examination Details

Candidate Answer Sheet 1

Instructions

Use a PENCIL (B or HB). Rub out any answer you wish to change using an eraser.

Part 1: Mark ONE letter for each question.

For example, if you think **B** is the right answer to the question, mark your answer sheet like this:

Parts 2, 3 and **4:** Write your answer clearly in CAPITAL LETTERS.

For Parts 2 and 3 write one letter in each box. For example:

Part 1				
1	A	B	C	D
2	A	B	C	D
3	A	B	C	D
4	A	B	C	D
5	A	B	C	D
6	A	B	C	D
7	A	B	C	D
8	A	B	C	D

Part 2

Do not write below here

9
10
11
12
13
14
15
16

Continues over ➡

CAE CPE R1

DP801

© UCLES 2018 Photocopiable

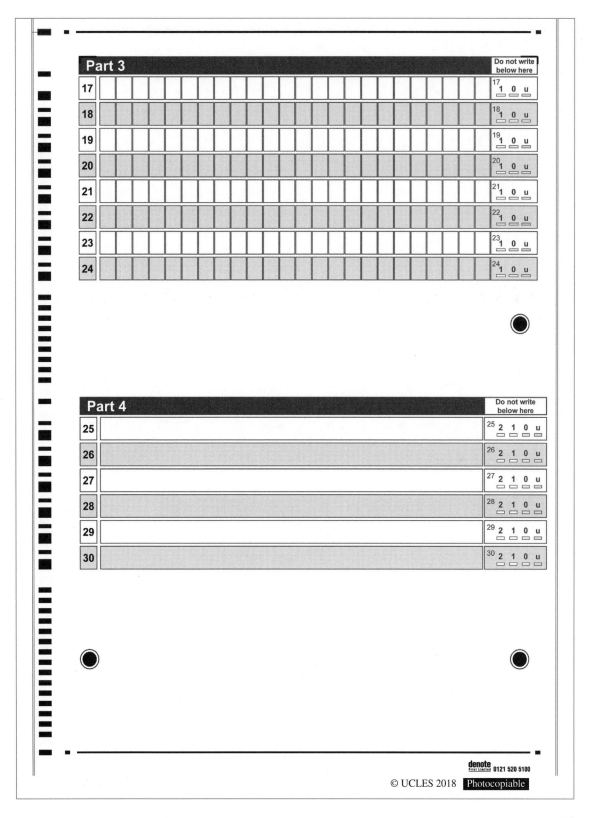

Part 3

Do not write below here

17
18
19
20
21
22
23
24

Part 4

Do not write below here

25
26
27
28
29
30

denote Print Limited 0121 520 5100

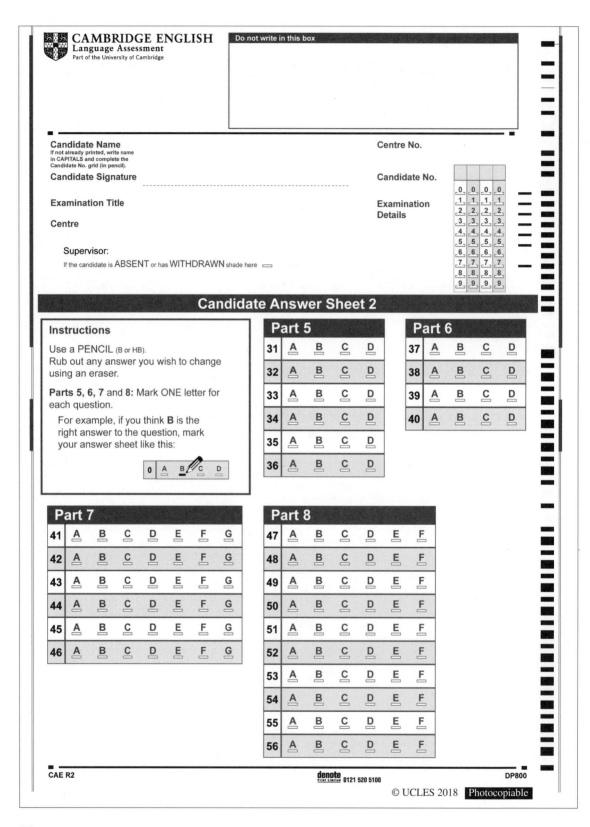

CAMBRIDGE ENGLISH
Language Assessment
Part of the University of Cambridge

Do not write in this box

Candidate Name
If not already printed, write name
in CAPITALS and complete the
Candidate No. grid (in pencil).

Candidate Signature

Examination Title

Centre

Supervisor:
If the candidate is ABSENT or has WITHDRAWN shade here

Centre No.

Candidate No.

Examination Details

Candidate Answer Sheet 2

Instructions

Use a PENCIL (B or HB).
Rub out any answer you wish to change
using an eraser.

Parts 5, 6, 7 and **8**: Mark ONE letter for
each question.

For example, if you think **B** is the
right answer to the question, mark
your answer sheet like this:

Part 5	A	B	C	D
31	A	B	C	D
32	A	B	C	D
33	A	B	C	D
34	A	B	C	D
35	A	B	C	D
36	A	B	C	D

Part 6	A	B	C	D
37	A	B	C	D
38	A	B	C	D
39	A	B	C	D
40	A	B	C	D

Part 7	A	B	C	D	E	F	G
41	A	B	C	D	E	F	G
42	A	B	C	D	E	F	G
43	A	B	C	D	E	F	G
44	A	B	C	D	E	F	G
45	A	B	C	D	E	F	G
46	A	B	C	D	E	F	G

Part 8	A	B	C	D	E	F
47	A	B	C	D	E	F
48	A	B	C	D	E	F
49	A	B	C	D	E	F
50	A	B	C	D	E	F
51	A	B	C	D	E	F
52	A	B	C	D	E	F
53	A	B	C	D	E	F
54	A	B	C	D	E	F
55	A	B	C	D	E	F
56	A	B	C	D	E	F

CAE R2

denote Print Limited 0121 520 5100

DP800

© UCLES 2018 Photocopiable

CAMBRIDGE ENGLISH
Language Assessment
Part of the University of Cambridge

Do not write in this box

SAMPLE

Candidate Name
If not already printed, write name
in CAPITALS and complete the
Candidate No. grid (in pencil).

Candidate Signature

Examination Title

Centre

Centre No.

Candidate No.

Examination
Details

Supervisor:

If the candidate is ABSENT or has WITHDRAWN shade here ▭

Candidate Answer Sheet

Instructions

Use a PENCIL (B or HB).
Rub out any answer you wish to change using an eraser.

Parts 1, 3 and **4:**
Mark ONE letter for each question.

For example, if you think **B** is the
right answer to the question, mark
your answer sheet like this:

Part 2:
Write your answer clearly in CAPITAL LETTERS.

Write one letter or number in each box.
If the answer has more than one word, leave one
box empty between words.

For example:

Turn this sheet over to start.

CAE L

DP803

© UCLES 2018   Photocopiable

Sample answer sheet: Listening

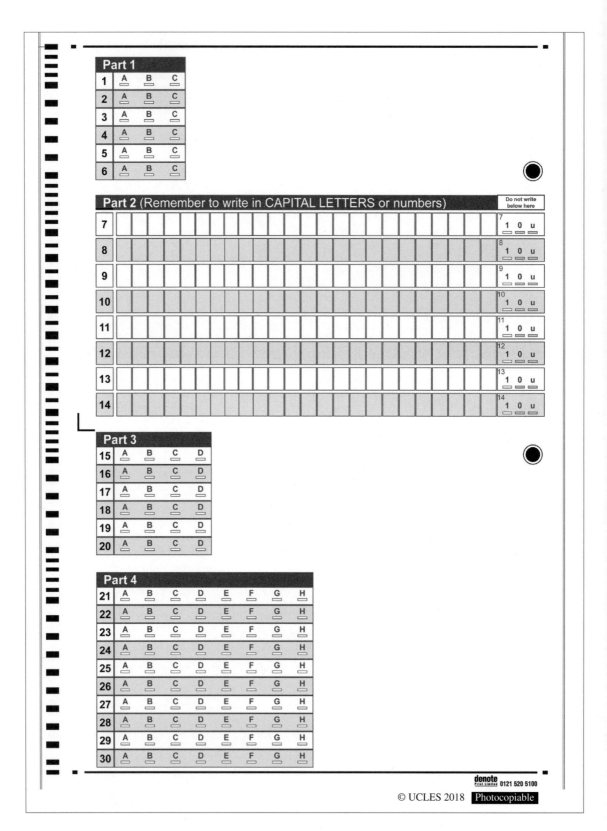

Acknowledgements

The authors and publishers acknowledge the following sources of copyright material and are grateful for the permissions granted. While every effort has been made, it has not always been possible to identify the sources of all the material used, or to trace all copyright holders. If any omissions are brought to our notice, we will be happy to include the appropriate acknowledgements on reprinting and in the next update to the digital edition, as applicable.

Key: TL = Top Left, CR = Centre Right, BL = Below Left.

Text Acknowledgements

Guardian News and Media Limited for the text on p. 16 adapted from 'Is London such a terrible place to live?' by Sam Jordison and Liz Hoggard, *The Guardian*, 23.08.2014. Copyright © 2014 Guardian News and Media Limited. Reproduced with permission; Syon Geographical Ltd. for the text on p. 18 adapted from 'Beavers create nitrogen sinks' by Laura Cole, Geographical website, 23.10.2015. Copyright © 2015 Syon Geographical Ltd. Reproduced with permission; James Willstrop for the text on p. 21 adapted from 'How should squash react as sport climbing and skateboarding are prioritised for the 2020 Olympics?' by James Willstrop, 30.09.2015. Copyright © 2015 James Willstrop. Reproduced with kind permission; Associated Newspapers Ltd for the text on p. 30 adapted from 'Learn to read the slow way' by Louise Heighes, *Metro*, 10.11.2010. Copyright © 2010 Associated Newspapers Ltd. Reproduced with permission; Guardian News and Media Limited for the text on p. 36 adapted from 'Charles Spence: the food scientist changing the way we eat?' by Amy Fleming, The Guardian, 24.09.2014. Copyright © 2014 Guardian News and Media Limited. Reproduced with permission; Independent Digital News & Media Ltd for the text on p. 40 adapted from 'Where the wild things are: Animal attraction in Costa Rica' by Mike Unwin, *The Independent*, 21.09.2012. Copyright © 2012 Independent Digital News & Media Ltd. Reproduced with permission; The Financial Times Ltd for the text on p. 43 adapted from 'How to identify a real Rembrandt?' by Bendor Grosvenor, *The Financial Times*, 10.10.2014. Copyright © 2014 The Financial Times Ltd. Reproduced with Permission; The Conversation Media Group Ltd. for the text on p. 58 adapted from 'The examined life: why philosophy needs to engage with the world, but hasn't' by Matthew Beard, The Conversation website, 08.06.2015. Copyright © 2015 The Conversation Media Group Ltd. Reproduced with permission; Guardian News and Media Limited for the text on p. 62 adapted from 'How I deal with the unbearable hypocrisy of being an environmentalist' by Madeleine Somerville, *The Guardian*, 05.04.2016. Copyright © 2016 Guardian News and Media Limited. Reproduced with permission; Guardian News and Media Limited for the text on p. 65 adapted from 'A girl growing up on film' by Anna Moore, The Guardian, 09.04.2016. Copyright © 2016 Guardian News and Media Limited. Reproduced with permission; Times Newspapers Limited for the text on p. 80 adapted from 'So why the long face?' by Tom Whipple, *The Times*, 31.08.2010. Copyright © 2010 Times Newspapers Limited. Reproduced with permission; Guardian News and Media Limited for the text on p. 84 adapted from 'Rain is sizzling bacon, cars are lions roaring: the art of sound in movies' by Jordan Kisner, *The Guardian*, 22.07.2015. Copyright © 2015 Guardian News and Media Limited. Reproduced with permission; Guardian News and Media Limited for the text on p. 87 adapted from 'The myth of the know-it-all scientist' by Dean Burnett, *The Guardian*, 01.03.2016. Copyright © 2016 Guardian News and Media Limited. Reproduced with permission.

Photo Acknowledgements

All the photographs are sourced from Getty Images.

p. C1 (TL): Dan Brownsword/Cultura; p. C1 (CR): Sharie Kennedy/Corbis; p. C1 (BL): Dylan Ellis/Photodisc; p. C2 (TL): Tom Merton/Caiaimage; p. C2 (CR): praetorianphoto/E+; p. C2 (BL): G. Baden/Corbis; p. C4 (TL): Prasit photo/Moment; p. C4 (CR), p. C5 (BL), p. C10 (BL): Hero Images; p. C4 (BL): Stuart Ashley; p. C5 (TL): Dan Dalton/Caiaimage; p. C5 (CR): Westend61; p. C7 (TL): f4foto/Alamy; p. C7 (CR): Hill Street Studios/Blend Images; p. C7 (BL): Heiner Heine/imageBROKER/Alamy; p. C8 (TL): allesalltag/Alamy; p. C8 (CR): Flying Colours Ltd/Photodisc; p. C8 (BL): OMG/The Image Bank; p. C10 (TL): rubberball; p. C10 (CR): Mint Images RF; p. C11 (TL): Aliyev Alexei Sergeevich/Cultura; p. C11 (CR): Caiaimage/Chris Ryan/OJO+; p. C11 (BL): Dave and Les Jacobs/Blend Images.

Visual materials for the Speaking test

- Why might the people be reading together?
- What might they do next?

1A

1B

1C

Visual materials for the Speaking test

- Why might the people be getting advice?
- How useful might the advice be?

1D

1E

1F

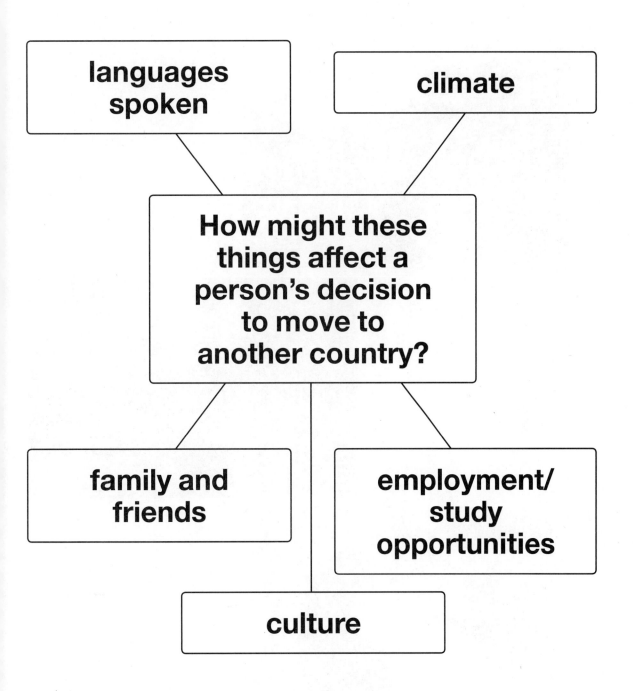

Visual materials for the Speaking test

- Why is water important to the people?
- How might they be feeling?

2A

2B

2C

- Why might the people be eating outside?
- How memorable might the experience be?

2D

2E

2F

2G

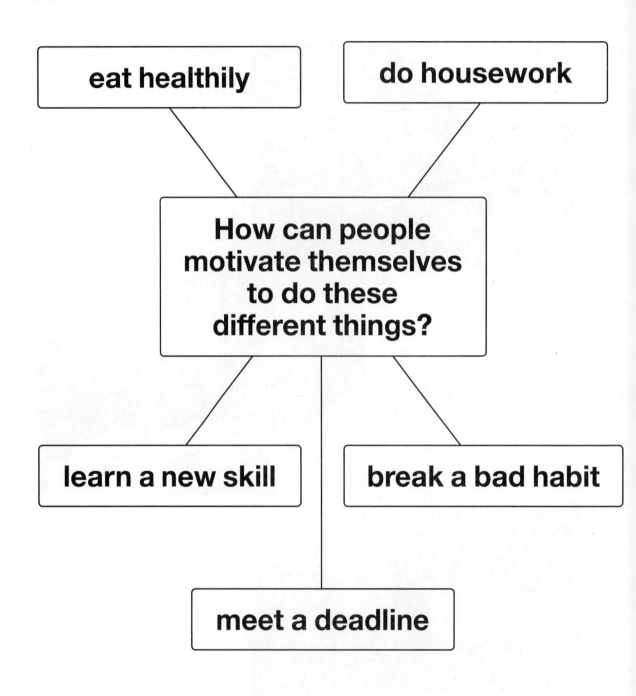

- Who could they be preparing the meal for?
- How might they be feeling

3A

3B

3C

- Why might these people be making a complaint?
- How could their complaint be dealt with?

3D

3E

3F

3G

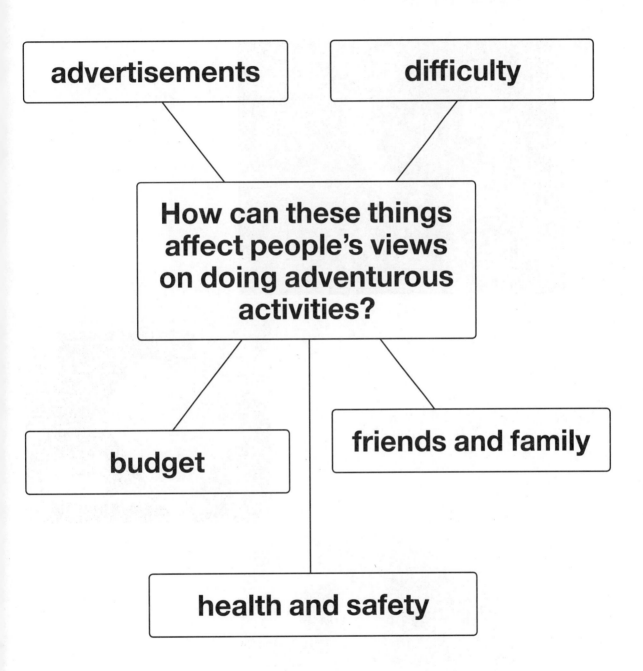

- What skills are needed to solve the problems?
- What difficulties may the people face?

4A

4B

4C

- Why might the people have decided to take photos in these situations?
- How carefully did they need to prepare?

4D

4E

4F

4G

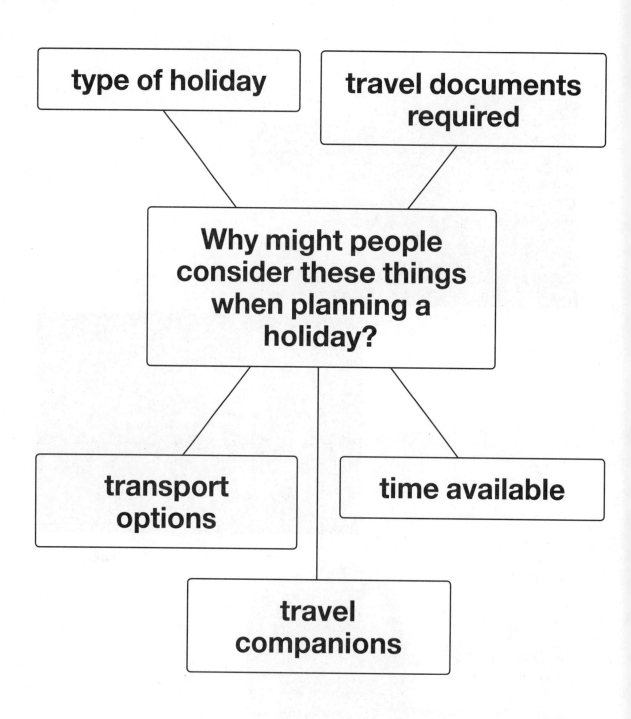

type of holiday

travel documents required

Why might people consider these things when planning a holiday?

transport options

time available

travel companions

Cambridge English

OFFICIAL EXAM PREPARATION MATERIALS

CAMBRIDGE.ORG/EXAMS

What do we do?

Together, Cambridge University Press and Cambridge English Language Assessment bring you official preparation materials for Cambridge English exams and IELTS.

What does *official* mean?

Our authors are experts in the exams they write for. In addition, all of our exam preparation is officially validated by the teams who produce the real exams.

Why else are our materials special?

Vocabulary is always 'on-level' as defined by the English Profile resource. Our materials are based on research from the Cambridge Learner Corpus to help students avoid common mistakes that exam candidates make.

Authentic examination papers: what do we mean?

PRETESTING

INVOLVING WRITING TEAMS AROUND THE WORLD

VALIDATION

PRACTICE PAPERS

← **SELECTION** →

LIVE EXAMS

Testbank

NOW ALSO AVAILABLE ONLINE IN Testbank

Practice makes perfect!

Testbank

Discover more
Official Preparation Materials

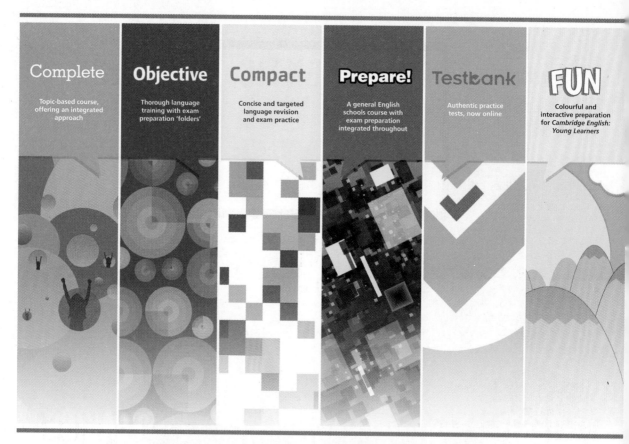

Complete
Topic-based course, offering an integrated approach

Objective
Thorough language training with exam preparation 'folders'

Compact
Concise and targeted language revision and exam practice

Prepare!
A general English schools course with exam preparation integrated throughout

Testbank
Authentic practice tests, now online

FUN
Colourful and interactive preparation for *Cambridge English: Young Learners*

Courses, self-study,
learner support

CAMBRIDGE.ORG/EXAMS